GALLAUDET

Friend of the Deaf

Also by Etta Degering:

WILDERNESS WIFE
The Story of Rebecca Bryan Boone

CHRISTOPHER JONES
Captain of the Mayflower

Gallaudet

FRIEND OF THE DEAF

ETTA DEGERING

Illustrated by Emil Weiss

Review and Herald Publishing Association
Washington, D.C. 20012

LIBRARY OF CONGRESS CATALOG CARD NUMBER 79-83923

Printed in U.S.A.

Foreword

Gallaudet: Friend of the Deaf is a biography I feel is long overdue. The work of Thomas Hopkins Gallaudet is a part of our American heritage. He pioneered the first permanent work for the deaf in America, founded the first school—the American School for the Deaf at Hartford, Connecticut in 1817. He gave to those handicapped by deafness both language and self-expression.

Hearing aids have changed the outlook for the deaf since his day and have altered methods of teaching, but they have not changed nor have they altered the story of how the work began. But this book is not a discussion of merits of teaching methods; it is the story of a remarkable man whose life and work left an indelible imprint on the American scene.

During the writing of the book, I became so well acquainted with Thomas and Sophia Gallaudet, and their family of eight, especially Edward, the youngest, that when I sent the manuscript to the publisher I felt lonely, as if cherished neighbors had moved away. Now, this family has come to live with you. I hope you will enjoy them as much as I have.

—THE AUTHOR

Boulder, Colorado
March 6, 1964

Acknowledgments

Many persons helped with the writing of this book. Elizabeth Yates, beloved New England author and lecturer at writers' conferences, suggested the original idea. "Why don't you write a book on Thomas Gallaudet, who did so much for the deaf?" she asked. "A companion book to the one you wrote on Louis Braille, who did so much for the blind."

Research on the book led me through many doors—school doors, library doors, doors to historical collections, and all of them opened willingly and wide.

At the Colorado School for the Deaf and the Blind, a residential school at Colorado Springs, Superintendent Armin G. Turechek and Principal James Kirkley welcomed me to the institution's library and classrooms. I received professional guidance and encouragement in my project.

A delightful day was spent with the hearing-handicapped children of the John Evans School of Denver, Colorado. This is a regular day school for the children of the neighborhood; it carries a specialized department of strictly oral instruction for boys and girls handicapped by varying degrees of deafness.

I visited Gallaudet College in Washington, D.C., the only college in the world devoted exclusively to hearing-handicapped youth. Mrs. Helen Cunningham of Public Relations took me on a tour of the campus. In the nursery school I saw tots of two and three years beginning to learn language with the help of hearing aids. At the upper end of the instructional curriculum is the collegiate department where I attended a class in college literature taught by Mr. Robert Panara, Associate Professor of English. Mr. Panara used the simultaneous method in lecturing—speech, though he heard not a word he said, finger-spelling, and signs. This multiple method of communication is used that the student may acquire the factual knowledge of college level by whichever means he can most readily grasp. Gallaudet College enjoys accredited standing.

A bronze statue on the college campus portrays Thomas Hopkins Gallaudet teaching nine-year-old Alice

Cogswell the letter A of the manual alphabet. I stood long minutes gazing at this sculptured representation of the beginning of education for the deaf of America. A photograph of the statue has inspired the cover of my book; for its use I thank Gallaudet College.

No book could be researched without the help of libraries and librarians. Mrs. Lucille Pendell, librarian of the Edward Miner Gallaudet Library on Gallaudet College campus, favored me with a private showing of the film, "The Life of Thomas Hopkins Gallaudet."

Mr. Henry J. Dubester, Chief of the General Reference and Bibliography Division of the Library of Congress, courteously extended to me the privilege of research in the Manuscript Division collection which includes material on both Thomas H. Gallaudet and his son, Edward M. Gallaudet, consisting of twenty-seven hundred pieces. I felt like an intruder as I read diaries and personal letters, inspected fading photographs and treasures, some of them a hundred and sixty years old.

Libraries of three universities lent a hand. Ohio State University opened its stacks to the research of its complete set of *American Annals of the Deaf*. Miss Jane Hill and Miss Judith Schiff of Yale Memorabilia Collections helped in the research of rules and entrance examinations of Yale College, 1802, the year of Thomas Gallaudet's enrollment. Miss Virginia N. Holbert, Librarian As-

ACKNOWLEDGMENTS

sistant of the University of Colorado, assigned me desk space for research and writing.

City librarians also helped. Miss Sylva Tanberg of Genealogy, Mrs. Wilma Aller of History and Biography, and Miss Phoebe Hayes, Director of Bibliographical Center of the Denver Public Library were tireless in making materials available. Miss Marcelee Gralopp, Children's Librarian of Boulder Public Library was especially helpful with background material.

Maxine Tull Boatner, Ph.D., author of *Voice of the Deaf,* and recognized authority of Gallaudet papers, read the manuscript and offered pertinent suggestions. Mrs. Boatner is the wife of Edmund D. Boatner, Superintendent of the American School at Hartford, Connecticut, the first permanent school for the deaf in America, and founded by Thomas Hopkins Gallaudet in 1817.

I wish to mention in my list of special assistance and inspiration Miss Rose Dobbs, Co-Editor of Books for Children and Young People at the David McKay Company in New York.

To each of the above named, and to the many others not named who contributed to the book, especially the hearing-handicapped boys and girls with their teachers who demonstrated lipreading and articulation, I wish to express sincere gratitude and appreciation.

—ETTA DEGERING

x

Contents

GALLAUDET

Friend of the Deaf

CHAPTER 1

Connecticut Boy

IT WAS mid-April, 1802, in Hartford, Connecticut. Thomas Gallaudet hitched his chair closer to the study table of the attic bedroom he shared with Charles, his next youngest brother. He bent his head closer to the Latin grammar. Classmates said the reason he always knew the answers was because he "smelled them out." Some day he would have glasses to correct the bothersome nearsightedness.

Smell or sight, in less than six months he had to give an account of his Latin, as well as Greek and arithmetic, in the Yale College entrance examinations. The time set for the examinations was nine o'clock, Tuesday morning, the third week in September.

He conjugated the more difficult verbs out loud, and

became aware of a mimic in the elm tree outside the open window. Blackie, the family pet crow, was trying his split tongue on the rhythmic clacking sounds. Every pause between present, past, or future tense of classic Latin was filled with bird Latin from the elm tree. Thomas laughed. "Be my good luck, Blackie."

Shouts from the yard below sent the old crow on some other cawing mission. Thomas reluctantly closed

the grammar. He hated to leave the assignment unfinished—hated to leave anything unfinished—but he had promised Charles to join a neighborhood game of fox and hounds. A visiting cousin from up-country, wise to the ways of foxes, would be the fox. The game promised to be a rugged run. Thomas didn't rate himself too high as a hound, being short, and "pindling" as his mother termed him.

When he joined the group in the yard, the fox had been given his vantage start. The hounds immediately took up the chase down tree-lined Prospect Street, past the Cogswell home, into the clearing beyond. Over plowed tobacco plots and hemp fields, leaping stone wall fences; through soggy river meadows; in and out of the woods, scattering a herd of hogs that rooted for chestnuts and acorns; up a rocky slope where sluggish rattlers might whirr right of possession, the hounds warily but doggedly pursued their fox.

An hour's run, and Thomas's breath came raspy and short; his lungs felt squeezed. On a wooded stretch he slipped out of the game, threw himself face down at the foot of a sugar maple, and waited for the ache to go out of his chest.

The baying of the hounds—a must in the game—as they attempted to out-run, out-smart the fox, grew fainter. He turned on his back better to follow the direction of the pack. Spears of last year's grass pricked through his tow cloth shirt; he inched along to a patch of sand.

Thomas resented the shirt, not because it was homespun, nor because it had faded from the deep blue of indigo dye to a grimy gray, but because it belonged to Charles, four years younger, and yet fit him fairly well. True, the buttons had to strain a bit, but to think he could wear it at all. . . . Why did he have to be such a puny undersized weakling? Would he never grow?

He forgot the hounds in his greater problem of size and strength. How did he come by his puniness, he puzzled as he had times without number? There was nothing puny or weak about his ancestry either in size or accomplishment. His merchant father, Peter Wallace Gallaudet, was strong and square-shouldered like his Huguenot father before him. Thomas sighed as he contrasted himself with Grandfather Gallaudet. When a boy his age, Grandfather had walked twenty miles to and from church, carrying his shoes to save leather, and singing most of the way.

His mother, Jane Hopkins Gallaudet, was but five generations removed from the Reverend Thomas Hooker who led the band of a hundred migrants with their cattle, blazing the first road from Boston to the Connecticut River, and staked out the town of Hart-

4

ford. She had named him Thomas Hopkins after her sea-captain father. Grandfather Hopkins had built the first brick house in Hartford, bringing the bricks and shingles from Holland in his sailing ship. No, there was no weakness in either side of his ancestry. He had a heritage to live up to. To remind himself he had once written in his diary:

> T. H. G. is the great-grandson of the
> great-granddaughter of Rev. Thomas Hooker.

Thomas didn't mind too much dropping out of the game, except that he *had* to drop out. Given the choice between a game and an afternoon in a hideout like the one under the sugar maple, with only his dreams and the birds to disturb the silence, he would choose the hideout every time, much to Charles's disgust.

Even when a boy of six or seven, his favorite pastime was to steal away into the woods or fields and dream about what he would do when he was grown up. Always at that age his fancy included making a lot of money, he didn't know quite how, and galloping through the country, maybe on a white horse, and giving the money away to people in need. He would pay off the farmers' debts, and free them from the dreaded debtors' prison. His mother should have one of the new iron cooking stoves, and his father—well, perhaps a new Bible; his was awfully worn.

As he dreamed he whistled, and when he came to the exciting parts he whistled louder and faster. "Yankee Doodle" was a good galloping song, although his Puritan mother didn't exactly favor it. She liked hymn tunes better.

As he grew older—he was now fourteen, had been since December 10—his dreams grew up, but he still dreamed. And then there were times, such as today under the sugar maple, when his dreams seemed to burst like soap bubbles, leaving only a damp emptiness. Would he never be strong? Never be able to fill a position of special usefulness?

His mother's only wish for her boys was that they become active Christian men. In what they were to be "active" she left to them. His father admonished, "Plan for service, not praise." What service?

Rested, Thomas sat up, and with his finger wrote in the cool yielding sand a list of possibilities—teacher, preacher, merchant, lawyer . . .

A twig snapped. The bushes parted. "Why'd you quit the game?" chided Charles. "It ain't half the fun—"

"Isn't, Charles." At least he could exchange grammar for shirts.

6

"It isn't half the fun," Charles repeated, "when you don't play."

Thomas broke off a branch of laurel and swept the sand smooth. "You fellows can out-run me any day in fox and hounds."

"Well, sometimes," admitted Charles, "but you know more tricks. You've got more *think*."

Thomas laughed but he was mightily pleased. More *think!* Maybe Charles had a point. Maybe that was the answer to his problem. Maybe he could make *think* balance what he lacked in size and strength. "Did you catch the fox?" he asked.

Charles shrugged. "Naw, he circled, and denned safe."

Six clear strokes of Center Church clock brought Thomas to his feet. Charles snapped his fingers as if the clock reminded him of an errand. "Father sent me to tell you it's time for supper and Bible reading. I had a hard time finding you, and now we're late."

Thomas slapped the sand from his clothes. Single file at a jog trot, he led the way by deer trail cutoff through the woods and clearing to Prospect Street. They had to stop for Dr. Cogswell to turn into his lane driving a span of grays hitched to a two-seated buggy. The doctor raised his tall beaver hat and called to them.

On up the path they raced to the weathered two-story home their father had purchased when he moved his business from Philadelphia to Hartford two years before. It was a large enough house in which the family, now numbering eight, could expand. The kitchen door opened to the good smell of beans baked with molasses, and fresh rye bread with caraway.

Jane Gallaudet, face flushed from the heat of the fireplace oven, turned to them. "Thomas, have you been dreaming again? Supper grows cold with waiting. Wash quickly." Although her mouth spoke sternly, Thomas saw a smile of understanding in her eyes.

The children took their places on the long benches at either side of the table, the older boys, Thomas and Charles, sitting next to Father at the head. Their mother sat opposite, handy to the pots on the hearth. They all bowed their heads above the pewter plates turned face down on the red checkered cloth, while their father asked the blessing. Except for the clatter of pewter against pewter, they ate in silence. It wasn't proper for children to speak in the presence of their elders unless first spoken to.

After supper came the Bible reading. Thomas thought their family probably did more Bible reading than any other in town. Father was certain that knowing the Good Book was a guarantee to his children growing

8

up "virtuous and vigorous." Whether the reading was voluntary or involuntary he was sure it would rub off on them. Thomas found his hero in the Apostle Paul, a small man who, in spite of his size and weak eyes, accomplished more than two or three ordinary men.

"Bedtime," Jane Gallaudet announced after prayers. Charles, already half asleep, dragged his feet toward the stairway. But Thomas, remembering the unfinished Latin, and the Greek and arithmetic not even touched, looked imploringly at his mother.

She sighed, then carefully measured off a length of candle and handed it to him. "This will give you two hours of study. After that you must sleep." She shook her head. "You are *so* pindling, Thomas."

CHAPTER 2

Height or High Standing

THE STAGECOACH left Hartford for New Haven daily at three o'clock in the morning, sometimes sooner, if the driver was unable to sleep. Father and Charles helped Thomas carry his luggage (he was allowed fourteen pounds free) to the Jeremy Addams tavern where the stagecoaches loaded. They walked by the light of a horn lantern.

The tavern was old, built in 1644, and stood on the same side of Main Street as Center Church. It not only served as inn and "victualing house" for travelers, but as post office and general gathering place for Hartford citizens. Thomas had often gone to the tavern to see the stagecoach come in, but his visits had always been in daylight. Now at two-thirty in the morning the

10

tavern had the appearance of a strange unfamiliar place.

A half dozen candles, smelling of tallow, cast phantom shadows on the irregular walls—distorted shadows of men with stilt legs and apple heads, or no legs, and noses as long as a white oak's reach. The eerie shadows seemed to conjure up ghosts of the tavern's past. Thomas knew his town's history, it was his family's early history. The ghost with the lengthy nose, was it not the nosey Governor Andros, sent by King James II more than a hundred years ago to govern all New England, and who demanded the forfeiture of Connecticut's charter?

In this very room, and on that very table the charter had lain when the lights were suddenly extinguished; and when they were relit the charter was gone. Thomas had many times climbed the oak on the Wyllys estate to peer into the hole where the charter had remained hidden until the withdrawal of the governor. He had probably gone there more often than any other Hartford boy. The Charter Oak was a good place to think and to dream.

Passengers yawned and complained of the early hours of stagecoaches. They were all strangers to Thomas, having come from Boston and towns along the Boston Post Road, and had spent the night at the tavern.

Thomas felt like a stranger himself with his new glasses, his first tailored suit of boughten cloth, and the "pudding cravate" that made him hold his head stiffly high with its many wrappings. He agreed with whoever it was that said the neck cloth must have been styled by someone who wished to hide a poulticed throat. He was secretly pleased with his new fur-felt hat. It made him feel taller, and the hatter hadn't been obliged to make it a smaller-than-average size, as the tailor had his suit.

The tavern door opened. "All aboard for New Haven, New York, and way stations," bellowed the stagecoach driver.

Father shook hands with Thomas as if he were a man. "Read your Bible, son. Write often. Do not fear the examinations. Your reward will be as you have studied."

Charles shoved a basket of lunch at him and mumbled something about, "Show them Yale fellows . . ."

Thomas didn't correct the grammar. There was a tight feeling in his throat. Maybe it was the choking neck cloth; besides, at the moment Charles seemed a most perfect brother, grammar and all.

The driver held his lantern high, urging everyone to "Step lively! Get aboard!" What Thomas saw of the outside of the stagecoach made him think of a huge box mounted on springs, with leather top, and leather side curtains to let down against the weather. The passengers entered from the front, climbing over the backless seats. The capacity was eleven persons besides the driver.

An old man moved over to make room for Thomas next to the outside. "Reckon ye'll like to look soon's it gets daylight."

At the crack of the whip and blast of the driver's horn, the horses lunged forward into the half-moon darkness down Main Street, over Little River (Park) bridge, taking the thirty-six mile turnpike south to New Haven. There would be fresh teams waiting at intervals of eighteen miles (stages) to keep up a rate of travel that assured New York passengers arrival on schedule the following day.

When morning broke, the familiar fox and hound country had been left behind, as also was Berlin with its brick kilns and tin factories. The maples and birches seemed to have lighted the day. Everywhere they blazed with red and gold. And because they were on all sides they appeared to go along with the stage. "No leaving the forest behind," someone observed.

At that the old man came out of his doze and sat up. "I recollect hearing," he said, "that when the white man come, a squirrel could travel across-t the hull state o' Connecticut, north t'south, east t'west, without a-comin' down out o' the treetops 'ceptin' at the river meadows."

"You've been this way before?" someone asked.

The old man chuckled. "Traveled this road nigh on twenty year ago. No graveled turnpike them days. Stage got stuck, and passengers had t' heave it out o' ruts and mudholes."

Thomas was glad for the talk. It made him forget "pending" examinations.

"I mind hearing," the old man continued, "that once-t the passengers balked on gettin' out in the mud. Whereat the driver he jist set down on a rock by the side of the road and lit his pipe. When the passengers axed what he intended to do about the perdicament they was in, he up an' told 'em. 'Since them hosses can't pull that kerrige out of that mudhole, and ye won't help, I'm a-goin' to wait till the mudhole dries up.' "

Everyone laughed at the tale, the old man loudest of all. Thomas was thankful he lived in the days of turnpikes. He wouldn't be much of a heaver. He was especially interested in the toll gates that stretched across the road. There would be four between Hartford and New Haven. On payment of twenty-five cents the gates swung open and let the stagecoach pass. The toll sign read:

14

25¢ for a carriage
6¼ ¢ for a one-horse wagon
1¢ for each animal driven in a herd
Church-goers and funerals free

The old man told Thomas that turnpikes got their name from the gates. "The fust ones was made by fastenin' four pikes parallel into a pole that turned," he explained.

Beyond Meriden there was the occasional wigwam or cabin of rough logs blackened with smoke. A stunted patch of corn or scraggly tree of wormy apples, and dirty half-naked children who stolidly stared at the stagecoach, proclaimed the poverty of the once powerful Mohegans. One of the passengers dismissed them with, "The cold of winter isn't thought of by the Indians until it is felt." But Thomas couldn't forget that they were once the owners of the hunting grounds from which they were now excluded.

The red cliffs of East Rock, the salty smell of seaweed, and forest of ship masts against Long Island Sound, told Thomas he was at the end of his journey. The stagecoach stopped at the tavern on New Haven Green. Thomas got off amid other passengers waiting to get on, and a horde of barefoot youngsters who had raced

15

the stage from the first blast of the driver's horn as it entered town.

"Good luck, young feller," the old man called back above the din as the stagecoach lurched forward still followed by the yelling, laughing children in spite of the dust clouds that rolled from its heavy wheels.

In the comparative quiet after the stage's departure Thomas took in his surroundings. He faced the sixteen-acre Green around which New Haven settlers had built their homes and places of business. The pioneers had used the Green as a safe pasture for their cattle at night, a market place by day, and drill ground for the militia. The State House and Meeting House, with its customary burying-ground, occupied the center of the Green. Close by were the old whipping post and pillory, relics of the strict discipline of the days when a man might be sentenced to stand with head and hands fastened in the pillory holes from "ye coming up of the sun to ye going down of the sun," for "unseemly conduct." The whipping post, where "stern-faced Elder Malbone publicly flogged his daughter, Martha, for having attended a house-warming with a young man of her acquaintance," was now gathering moss from disuse.

Thomas looked long and hard at the west border of the Green. Facing it was Yale College, surrounded by tall fan-shaped elms and a low board-rail fence. Its three long identical buildings presented an almost solid brick front. Within those walls he would make his home during the next few years—he hoped. Within them he would take the entrance examinations, and know his fate, during the next three days.

Collecting his luggage, he took one of the diagonal paths across the Green and walked with a boldness he did not feel. On which door, he wondered, should he knock—each building had two doors—and then he saw an open door. The open door seemed to say, "Welcome! We have been expecting you."

He entered Connecticut Hall.

Yale chapel clock, sadly out of tune, chimed the hour of nine A.M. Thomas felt as out of tune as the clock and miserably out of place, as he sat in the reception room of President Timothy Dwight's office, waiting his turn to begin the round of entrance examinations. He looked at the other entrants. Did he appear as dull as they?

He gazed at the portraits on the wall, portraits of former presidents of Yale College. They looked down at him with dour, solemn, accusing faces, echoing his father's words, "Your reward will be as you have studied." Had he studied hard enough? He tried to recall rules in arithmetic but his mind refused to concentrate; Greek Testament translation was fuzzy; Latin verbs . . .

Like a flash from nowhere he heard a harsh old crow's voice attempting Latin verbs from the top of an elm tree. He grinned at the memory. The grin relaxed his tense muscles and smoothed the goose pimples on his arms. When he again looked about him, the presidents seemed less solemn, the students less dull. Blackie *was* "good luck."

Until five o'clock he went from one examiner to another and answered questions, both oral and written. Then came the anxiety of waiting for the results. Minutes dragged like hours until he was handed the examination returns.

He unfolded the report and, trembling, read the sheet. ". . . accepted into the Sophomore year of Yale College . . ." It couldn't be true. His new glasses must be playing tricks. He read again. *Sophomore* year, it was. He had skipped Freshman year. He wanted to shout, turn hand springs, anything!

Thomas completed his matriculation. He had met his professors and the tutors of the sophomore class. He had started down the long hall of college education by way of Roman History, Euclid, Greek, Latin, and his favorite subject, English. Later the scholastic hall would widen with the addition of Chemistry, Astronomy, Logic, Philosophy.

But before proceeding further down the scholastic hall, he found he must stop, memorize, and begin to practice the *Book of Rules and Customs*. Yale College, it seemed, was regulated and run by rule. The bulletin board announced that Senior So-and-so would read and explain the book of rules to all new students from the pulpit of Long Gallery in Connecticut Hall at four o'clock.

Thomas took his seat as the senior brought the assembly to order with repeated whacks of a hardwood gavel. "The first rule concerns hats" announced the upper classman who obviously enjoyed his task.

All undergraduates are forbidden to wear their hats (unless in stormy weather) in the front door yard of the President's or Professor's house, or within ten rods of the person of the President, eight rods of the Professor, and five rods of the Tutor.

Thomas decided that, being nearsighted as to distances, and not yet used to his glasses, he had best go hatless except "in stormy weather," but changed his mind on hearing the last part of the rule:

Freshmen are forbidden to wear their hats in the College yard ... until May Vacation.

If he didn't wear his hat he would be taken for a freshman, and freshmen held the least enviable position at Yale. Perhaps a part of his education would have to include learning to estimate distances.

Next came the rules of fagging. The senior cleared his throat and read with emphasis:

Freshmen are obliged to perform all reasonable errands for any superior ... When called, they shall attend and give a respectful answer; and when attending on their superior, they are not to depart until regularly dismissed.

There were many rules governing the hapless freshman. He must remain standing in the presence of his superiors until "bidden to sit." Before entering a gate or door belonging to the college, he must observe whether any superiors were coming to same. If any were coming within three rods he must not enter without signal to proceed. He was forbidden to walk with a cane. ... How lucky, Thomas thought, to have skipped freshman year. As to errands, he would do his own.

The senior droned on. Rule of Fines—

One penny for absence of undergraduate from prayers

One half penny for tardiness

Four to six pence for absence from one's chamber during study period

One shilling for picking open a lock—two for second offence

One shilling for jumping out of windows . . .

"President Dwight," whispered a New Haven boy, "has tried to do away with both fagging and fines, but the tutors have so far successfully opposed him." Thomas heartily approved of President Dwight's stand. Both rules, he felt, were unfair, especially the rule of fines. A rich boy could do much as he pleased in college as long as he paid his fines.

Rules, rules, and more rules, before the book was emphatically closed and the reader looked his audience in the eye with an expression that defied objections.

The rule that nettled Thomas most was the rule forbidding any student to go farther than two miles off the campus without special permission from the President. He held that fields, woods, and beach were made for roaming, and the President wasn't always easy to find. The rule that concerned him least was the one forbidding the "kicking of a football in the college yard."

He wasn't football material. Outdoor activity for him practically ended with quoits and hikes in summer, skating and tobogganing in winter. Anyway, football was not *the* competitive sport of Yale in 1802. Debating was the top competition, and he was definitely interested in it. Words fascinated him. He had a way with them. But how would he do in a debate?

There were weekly skirmishes between small debating teams as tryouts for the regular college teams. Leaders chose sides from among the new students. Thomas was one of the last chosen, and he knew why. It was the same at home in choosing for fox and hounds; the younger boys were always chosen last. His size was against him.

Debating was like fox and hounds in other ways, he decided. Debaters, like hounds, had to anticipate the intentions of the fox-opponents, and outwit them. He was supposed to be good in the outwitting part of the game—at least Charles thought so—but in a debate ...

His chance finally came. The debate was wound up in a multitude of meaningless words like the trick of a sly fox misleading the hounds on a devious path intending to backtrack up the creek and laugh from behind a thicket as the hounds yelped by.

The captain of the team indicated Thomas for rebuttal. Thomas had the feeling that he thought the debate lost anyway; might as well give that stripling from Hartford a chance.

He felt his knees tremble, heard his voice quaver; his mouth was chip-dry. Was he going to fail? Have to drop out? He forced himself to forget the eyes turned on him, concentrated on the fox laughing from behind his thicket of words, and disclosed his devious intentions. With a twist of words he turned the laugh on his opponent and scored for his team.

The Brothers of Unity invited Thomas to join their literary society and debating team. He wrote a book of debates for the group, giving both sides of the argument. He wrote with a sharpened quill on unlined paper, the lines of writing marching across the page as straight as his line of thought. He wrote on the favorite debated topics of the day:

> Have Brutes Reason?
> Ought Homicide by Dueling Be Punished by
>   Death?
> Should Dictates of Conscience Invariably Be
>   Followed?
> Are Theaters Beneficial?

On the last page of "Are Theaters Beneficial?" he added in disgust: "Written in great haste. If examined it will be found to contain but four or five arguments." He gathered the pages together and bound them into a book with marbled covers. Thomas became president of the Brothers of Unity at their next election.

Every month he appreciated the leadership of President Timothy Dwight more and more. He wrote his father, "You will be pleased to know that the leading educator in America learned to read the Bible when he was four, and has read it daily since."

For a full month President Dwight lectured on "Is the Bible a true book?" As a result there was "a great religious revival among the students," written up in the annals of Yale as the outstanding event of Yale's one-hundredth anniversary.

Sophomore, Junior, Senior! The years winged by. Changes had taken place at Yale College: fagging had been done away with, self-respect and loyalty substituted for fines. The "new and elegant" library called Lyceum had been completed. When summing up the three years Thomas used the word "satisfying."

The 1805 graduating class of forty-two members had been posted for September Commencement. Thomas was listed as one of the six who would graduate with the honor of an oration.

It was rumored the faculty was having difficulty deciding on the valedictorian: that Thomas Gallaudet and Gardiner Spring had tied in scholarship and merit. Interest and speculation mounted!

Was it possible that he, Thomas Gallaudet, the youngest in the class, might have the highest honor? He must not let himself covet. All his boyhood he had been taught that to covet was the most sinful of sins. But just suppose . . .

And then President Dwight, sponsor of the senior class, called him to his office and apologetically explained that since Gardiner was several inches taller, the faculty had voted him as having the highest standing. "But," he hastened to add, "you shall be Latin Salutatorian, and have the additional honor of speaking with five of your classmates in the dialogue, 'Timophanes, or the Tyrant of Corinth.' "

Thomas bowed respectfully. "Thank you, sir. Thank you for everything." But he made a mental note to write Charles that *think* didn't always make up for lack in size, that sometimes it took height along with high-standing to capture top honors.

CHAPTER 3

"To Every Man His Work"— What Was His?

AFTER graduation Thomas entered the firm of the Honorable Chauncy Goodrich in Hartford to study law. One of his instructors was the Chief Justice of Connecticut. Thomas was prompt, his assignments always completed, instructors spoke words of commendation, but a year's trial proved that his health could not stand the long hours of indoor concentration. As in the long ago game of fox and hounds he had to drop out.

Again he didn't feel too much regret except that he hated to leave anything unfinished. Law, he found, didn't quite measure up to his ideal of a profession. It wasn't something he wanted to spend his whole life at, or put his whole heart into. The long formal *whereases* tacked on to everything he wrote were like skeletons of dry bones. He liked to be more original, use his own words. But to what should he turn? "To every man his work," his father kept assuring him. What was his?

Perhaps a year at home, studying English on his own, would build up his strength and give him time to decide on the future. His parents were sympathetic to his problem. Charles, who was serving an apprenticeship with a Hartford engraver, was glad to have his roommate back. To his younger brothers and sisters he meant stories, romps, and walks. "Thomas has a way with the young ones," said his mother, who also saw to it that this unaccountably frail son of hers had plenty of quiet time for study and rest.

Thomas enjoyed putting words together into essays, discourses, and debates. He wrote articles and editorials for the *Hartford Courant*. He contributed to *The Children's Magazine*, first juvenile periodical in America, also published in Hartford. He was called on for speeches and orations.

Weeks, months, a year passed—but no sun came up on his future's horizon to light the way. The days for him became gloomy and drab, uncertain and insecure. He covered up his discouragement with an assumed gayety. Only his diary knew of the misery and doubts that plagued him, that he doubted himself, doubted his fellows, and sometimes almost doubted God.

To feel this way he knew was wrong, but how did one go about changing one's feelings? "If only feelings could be discarded like boots," he wrote, "and a new set purchased," he would be willing to pay "a handsome price."

It was New Year's Eve, the time for resolutions. What resolutions should he make? He stood by the window of his room, but instead of looking out at the candle-lighted windows appearing one by one against the elm-silhouetted twilight, he was looking within himself and seeing his faults. Minute by minute he became more discouraged, more depressed.

The striking of Center Church clock interrupted his thoughts. He counted the hour. Six o'clock. Time for supper and—he turned from the window—Bible reading. He recalled that his father always vowed Bible reading would make a man "virtuous and vigorous." There was nothing he would like better right now than to feel both virtuous and vigorous. A new thought came to him. Perhaps the results were in direct proportion to the amount of reading. He knew what his New Year's resolution would be.

After supper, with his Bible on the table beside him, he wrote in his diary:

New Year's Eve, January 1808
I resolve that . . . I will read in the Scriptures thrice
a day . . .
I will pray morning, noon, and night . . .
I will attend divine service every week . . .

His diary took on a brighter tone the following month.

Spring brought Thomas an official-looking envelope by stage post. It was postmarked New Haven. Wondering, he broke the seal. Inside was a letter from President Dwight informing him that he had been elected to the position of tutor at Yale College with the privilege of working towards his Master's Degree. Would he accept?

Would he? He could think of nothing he would like better. He was especially pleased when he learned that a classmate and distant kinsman, Edward Hooker, had also been elected to tutorship. Instead of being led as when students, they would now be leading.

Yale College had grown in both buildings and enrollment. The Green seemed greener. The elms were taller. Thomas was interested in the new bi-weekly paper, *Literary Cabinet*. It would be a challenge to him through his pupils.

Daily, Thomas reminded himself of the days when he had been a student, and the kind of tutor he had appreciated. He endeavored to be that tutor. To his students he became "the little tutor who knows all the answers." Not only answers to Euclid, science, and English, but answers to their personal problems. They confided in him.

Little did they realize that their tutor was having his own problems. His diary, alone, knew about the blue days—days when he was sure he "hadn't yet found the way called Christian," when he was sure he was on "the road to perdition." He felt he was frivolous to a fault; that he often let his sense of humor run away with him, become plain foolishness. Friends depended on him to keep their parties from becoming dull. He could make people laugh, and people liked to laugh.

The climax came at an evening social when he recklessly joined in the hilarity. A drink and a laugh! A drink and a laugh! Until for the first time in his life Thomas drank too much and had to be helped home.

The remorse, the shame afterward! He couldn't rest until he had taken the stagecoach to Hartford and confessed before the officers of Center Church, the church he hoped soon to join, what he had done. To see the look in the face of his father, who was treasurer of the church, a look of forgiveness and at the same time confidence, was a cure for all time. Never again did Thomas take a drink of anything that even resembled intoxicating liquor.

He felt that his confession in Center Church, with its new steeple reaching above the elms, had been heard "up there," but that the line was not quite clear between him and his forefathers until he had visited the grave of the Reverend Thomas Hooker in the cemetery back of the church. Then once more he could hold up his head and say, "I am the great-grandson of the great-granddaughter of the Reverend Thomas Hooker."

Two years Thomas enjoyed his work as tutor at Yale College. He earned his M.A. degree with the honor of an oration. But once again his health rebelled. He *had* to drop out. This time with great regret.

As the stagecoach swayed and jounced its way north on the turnpike, Thomas tried to think of other things besides himself. He watched the countryside go by, and was impressed with the many new clearings. The farmers, he observed, used the trees for houses and barns and fuel. They built their fences from the rocks and stones which, numerous to begin with, seemed to multiply each year as if they boiled up from some great kettle below. As a result the gray stone walls grew longer and longer, extending over the ridges, dipping down into the gullies, taping the whole countryside together.

Passengers commented on the rocky soil. A man laughed. "Connecticut sheep, they say, have pointed noses from nibbling grass between the rocks."

"Look at those granite boulders," observed another, "brought down by a glacier from the White Mountains. Some poor fellow's trying to grow crops between them. He'll never make it."

"A rock," said the first passenger, "has put an end to many a Connecticut man's dream, and I don't mean his tombstone, either."

Thomas winced. He had dreams. Would a rock end his dreams? The rock of frail health? No, the passenger was wrong. Rocks didn't always end dreams; sometimes they helped. He had read of a young man named Jacob who used a rock for a pillow, and that night he dreamed the most encouraging dream of his life. The boulders in the field might help the farmer to decide on some other type of work, something more suitable or better for him.

Following his own reasoning, Thomas decided to try a different type of work. After a rest at Hartford he signed a commission with a New York firm to travel as Yankee trader in the states of Ohio and Kentucky. The outdoor life should be a tonic to his health.

He bought a brown mare and loaded his packs—

buttons, pins, needles, clocks, tinware, screws, brass
wire, gun parts, knives, ribbons—all products of Connecticut factories. Fresh supplies would be shipped to
him by flatboat down the Ohio River.

Thomas kept a diary of his trip in a handmade three-
by-four-inch notebook that would slip easily into his
shirt pocket. In it he faithfully recorded the mileage
and weather each day:

> *Only twelve miles today, roads muddy from the
> drizzling rain.*
> *Sunny today, trail good, made thirty-four miles.*

The farther he rode into Kentucky, the more royal
the welcome. He was the backwoodsman's first contact
for many a month with the world outside his bluegrass–
forest state. He found the Kentuckians hardly knew
whether they lived under President Jefferson or President Madison. Always he was invited to "set a spell."
There would be "vittles" for him and grass "a-plenty"
for his horse.

As Thomas sat in the proffered best chair, handmade
from the forest, and talked with his host, the housewife
would add to the ever-present black iron kettle, swing
it on its crane into the fireplace, and stir the coals into
a blaze. Deftly she would beat up a batch of journey

cake (corn bread) and put it to bake on a board leaned against the fireplace bricks.

The children, who at first hid, gradually crept nearer. Thomas finally brought them close to him by a ventriloquist trick that was a favorite with his small brothers and sisters. Taking a piece of charcoal from the fireplace he drew the face of a grandmother on his left hand. He made her a granny's cap with his handkerchief, and then with his thumb slightly bent against forefinger for a mouth, he made granny tell stories and ask all sorts of questions. Ventriloquist Granny, he called the puppet. By the time the "vittles" were ready the children were laughing and begging for more stories.

The best and perhaps the only china plate, one that had belonged to the housewife's mother in England, and carried in a roll of bedding over the Cumberland Trail into Kentucky, was placed on the sawhorse table for him. There was buffalo or deer stew, turnip greens, and journey cake with wild honey. Thomas ate with an outdoor appetite.

Then came the opening of the packs. The family gathered around and admired the display as if it had been let down from heaven. Always the man needed gun parts and the woman needles. And if they could possibly manage they bought a clock.

"The sun, hit is unsartin," explained the man for such

an extravagance, " 'specially when hit rains." Winding
the clock, and evidently satisfied that the loud tick
guaranteed performance, he grinned at his wife. Then
turning to Thomas, "My woman here has been a-pinin'
for the tick of a clock ever sence we come t' Kaintuck.
We'uns will take hit."

[A salesman who later traveled in that part of Kentucky wrote, "In nearly every cabin, even if the family
didn't own a chair, I found a Connecticut clock."]

With directions to the next clay-chinked cabin
Thomas and mare took to the trail. However, if it were
late in the day, he would be urged to stay the night,
sleeping in the corner pole bed while its usual occupants
slept on a bearskin on the floor. After a breakfast of
grits and gravy with bear bacon, Thomas then set out,
the sun warming his back, and the remembered hospi-
tality warming his heart.

At the end of the season Thomas was as brown as the
mare, and he felt fine. When he figured his accounts the
company's funds were intact, but as for himself, he
hadn't done so well. He hadn't been able to resist the
wistful look in children's eyes as they gazed at ribbons,
jackknives or trinkets, nor the apparent need of the
mother for a pan with no funds to buy. Many things
found their way from pack to cabin under the guise of

premium or bonus, since all Kentuckians were "dead sot agin pay for entertainin' strangers."

To replenish his funds Thomas wrote "LAWYER" on a board and nailed it over a cabin door in a river town. He quoted law to settle claims and disputes, and drew up legal papers. His clients, rawboned giant men, who seemed to have difficulty mustering enough words to ask their questions, stood amazed as the little lawyer quoted long paragraphs of law from memory and "spouted argiments." A group usually came with each client just to hear "that thar Yankee orate."

Back in New York, Thomas signed a further contract with the business firm for which he had traveled to work in their city establishment. Had he at last found his life work? Was business to be his career? It was his father's. Could he put his whole heart into it?

Thomas's diary is silent for more than a year, and then in black ink, written in the familiar hand:

Andover, Massachusetts
Sunday Morning, Jan. 12, 1812

I joined the day before yesterday the divinity college in this place . . . Oh! Thou God of all truth, if my purpose in devoting myself to the ministry be any but the right one . . . show me . . . my intended pursuit. . . .

36

Business had proved to be a repetition of his experience in law. Neither his health nor his heart agreed with it.

Thomas was now twenty-five. He entered into study to become a minister with mind and soul. He spoke in neighboring churches and was well received. Before acquiring his diploma, in September 1814, flattering offers of parishes had come to him, offers he dared not accept. Again it was a health problem. Still he clung to the promise, "To every man his work," and he was sure the work part of the promise didn't mean a half job.

And then it happened! It was while he was home on vacation from Andover College that he found his work, or rather, it found him. And with the work, miracle of miracles, he also found he had a spirit within him strong enough to do it!

CHAPTER 4

"No School for the Deaf Ones"

THOMAS lounged in the July sun on the porch steps of the family home on Prospect Street. He was on vacation from Andover Theological Seminary trying to build up health and energy for the remaining weeks of his ministerial course.

He was pleasantly tired. During the early afternoon he had visited some of his favorite boyhood haunts and hideouts. The clearing, he found, had pushed back the forest, and the deer trail was overgrown from disuse, but the sugar maple had broadened its place on the hill. The river meadows waved their tireless green as always. The Charter Oak still stood, but for how long was a question. Once a mighty council tree of the Pequot Indians, and then keeper of the white man's charter, it now resembled a tired old warrior who might not answer next spring's roll call.

Thomas yawned and stretched. It was good to be home. He now held the prestige of being the oldest of twelve brothers and sisters; ten of them living. Charles was doing well as an engraver. He discussed with Thomas the advisability of accepting an invitation from the wealthy William H. Imlay to become a junior partner. Brother William wrote from Yale that he had decided on medicine as a career. Did Thomas approve?

Why did these brothers confide in him, ask his advice, when he had always had, and still had, such difficulty deciding his own work? Just this week he had received a letter from "North Parish" of Portsmouth, New Hampshire, inviting him to take charge, after his graduation, of its pulpit about to be vacated. The earnest request was signed by men of prominence, among them, Daniel Webster who had just commenced his career in Congress. Thomas knew that when he returned to Andover, he would have to write declining the offer because his health was such he could not fill the office properly. He sighed. Was he always to be the proverbial square peg unable to fill a round hole?

His thoughts were interrupted by his younger brothers and sisters who, with playmates, came trooping around the corner of the house, laughing and panting from some running game. He watched them form a circle on the grass to rest up with a guessing game. He became aware of one girl who sat apart from the group, her face turned wistfully toward them. There was something different about this girl. It wasn't her pink ruffled dress, nor her blond curls, nor her pretty face—but wait, it *was* her face. Her face was the cherubic face of a child of four while her size indicated she must be twice that age.

He called Theodore, his nine-year-old brother, from the circle. "Who is the little girl sitting over there by herself?"

Teddy looked in the direction he indicated. "Her? Why, don't you know? She's Alice Cogswell. Doc Cogswell's girl—lives next door."

"Why doesn't she play with the group?"

Teddy shrugged. "She can't. She's deaf and dumb."

Deaf and dumb. So that was it. "Bring her to me. Maybe I can think of a game she can play. She looks lonesome."

Teddy ran over to Alice, made a sweeping motion "to come," left her with Thomas, and hurried back to the circle.

Thomas smiled and patted the step beside him. Alice sat on the very edge like a pink butterfly—if there are pink butterflies—ready to take flight.

Now what? His granny story was of no use here. College B.A. and M.A. degrees offered no solution. He thought fast. With all his soul Thomas longed to open this child's "silent prison," find a way for her to be one with the other children. Her need was some way of conversing. Could she be taught to write, he wondered.

Picking up his hat, the only thing he had at hand, he gave it to her, and stooping, wrote *hat* in the sand of the path.

Alice looked at him blankly. The marks in the sand meant nothing to her. Again and again, Thomas handed her the hat and wrote *hat* in the sand. He pointed to the writing and then to other things and shook his head. He pointed to the hat and nodded vigorously.

Her forehead puckered. She was trying to understand. She looked from the hat to the writing. What did those marks in the sand have to do with the thing she held in her hand?

Thomas breathed a prayer.

Finally a glimmer of light shone in the hazel eyes. Her forehead smoothed. She smiled and nodded.

For the first time in her life, Alice understood that things had names, names that could be written in the sand. She indicated that she wanted to write. Thomas helped her until she could write *hat* from memory.

He turned the writing into a game. When Alice wrote *hat*, he offered her his handkerchief, a twig, a stone. She laughingly shook her head until he held out the hat.

Suddenly Alice sobered. She pointed to herself and then to the sand. She wanted to write the word that meant herself. When Thomas wrote *Alice*, she again pointed to herself and looked at him questioningly. He nodded. Satisfied, she began practicing her name.

She was still working on it when Dr. Cogswell drove into his lane. Immediately she was all excitement. She took Thomas by the hand, motioned for him to bring the hat, and pulled him along with her.

When they reached the lane Dr. Cogswell had turned his team over to the stable boy and was coming toward the house. Alice ran to him. Thomas saw by the embrace how close were this father and daughter. Alice tugged at her father to come. Evidently thinking Alice wanted him to meet her friend, he smiled and shook hands with Thomas.

But Thomas knew what Alice was about. He handed her his hat. She passed it to her father and dropped to her knees. In the roadway she wrote *hat* in the dust.

Thomas would never forget the look in Dr. Cogswell's eyes—astonishment, joy, and love—all mixed up with tears that wouldn't stay back. He tried to hug his little daughter but she would have none of it. She hadn't finished. She pointed to herself and began to write. She managed the *Ali* but could go no farther, and held up her hand to Thomas for help; together they completed her name. Now she was ready for the hug and well-done pat.

Dr. Cogswell told Thomas that they had tried, but never had they been able to get it across to Alice that things had names. He invited Thomas into the house. He wanted to hear how he had succeeded in teaching this fact to their daughter, "especially dear to them because of her handicap." He told Thomas Alice's story:

She was two years old and learning to talk when she was taken sick with the dread spotted fever. The sickness had left her with no hearing at all, and it wasn't long before she had forgotten how to speak the few words she had learned. Now that she had reached the age of nine, he and Mrs. Cogswell were greatly perplexed about what to do.

"There are no schools for deaf children in America," he said. "It seems that we shall be obliged to send Alice either to the school in England or the one in Scotland where it is reported that deaf children learn not only to read and write but to speak with the voice as do hearing children. Oral schools they are called."

45

The doctor paused and looked thoughtfully out of the window. "She is so small to be sent so far away. We have put off the day." He looked hopefully at Thomas. "Since you have opened the door for her to written language, would it be possible for you to teach her more, and show us how? We then could wait until she is older to send her away to school."

"I will be glad to do what I can," Thomas assured him, "but I have no training."

Dr. Cogswell went to his library and took down the two volumes of a book, called the *Théorie des Signes*. "This is a book I sent for from the Royal Institution for the Deaf and Dumb in Paris. It is written in French by the Abbé Sicard, head of the school. The students at this school converse by means of finger-spelling, signs, and gestures. The abbé claims it is the natural language of the deaf."

The doctor leafed through the book. "The greater part of the book lists *signs*, a sign for a word, much as a dictionary gives definitions, but in the back is the manual alphabet. You will note that the letters of the alphabet are formed by different positions of the fingers, using but one hand." He passed the book to Thomas.

This was very interesting. The deaf could talk with their hands, spell words with their fingers. "Have you

tried to teach Alice finger-spelling?" he asked the doctor.

"With no more success than our efforts at teaching her writing. She imitates our motions as a sort of game, but they mean nothing to her. Would you care to take the book home and see what you could do with this method?"

Thomas assured him he would be glad to, and then asked, "Are there many deaf-mutes in Connecticut?"

"Eighty-four, according to the ministers' census of 1812," said the doctor. "I figure that means there are at least four hundred in New England, and more than a thousand in America."

Thomas left for home after setting a time for Alice to come for a lesson the next day. He stopped at the house next door only long enough to leave the book. He walked on and on, thinking over what he had just heard: eighty-four deaf in Connecticut, four hundred in New England, a thousand in America! No schools! No education for them! No way of telling them the gospel story!

He thought of the happiness of Alice on learning just two words. What would it be if she could read a book! If only there were a school for her in America . . . for all those other deaf ones.

A robin, singing its rain song from the topmost branch

of a chestnut tree, seemed to catch the flow of his thought, and plaintively chir-r-ruped:

No school for the deaf ones! No school!
No school for the deaf ones! No school! No school!

Thomas walked until late. Before returning home, he had outlined a plan of work for himself, for the next year at least. When he finished at Andover, he would "preach occasionally and travel considerably" searching out the deaf, beginning near Hartford. He would try to bridge the chasm of language, and help them to to help themselves towards a knowledge of things.

Before Alice arrived the next day for class, Thomas made out a list of words to teach her, and then he tore it up. He would let Alice lead the way. As she felt the need of a word he would teach her to write and finger-spell it. *Hat*, she had already learned to write. Today she would spell it on her fingers:

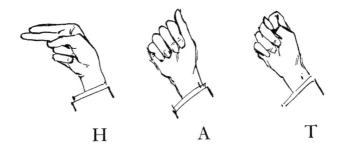

H   A   T

Thomas was astonished at how rapidly Alice learned. Sometimes more than twenty words at a lesson, and the next day she remembered them. His brothers and sisters wanted to learn the new way of talking. Alice was delighted to be in a class. They talked to each other by spelling words on their fingers and by signs.

Signs were fun. They were like drawing pictures in the air, and sometimes a short cut to spelling, like the word elephant. To sign elephant one simply swooped his hand downward as if along an elephant's trunk. The sign for boy—hand reaching upward as if grasping the bill of a cap; girl—hand closed, with the thumb tracing an imaginary bonnet string from cheek to under the chin.

Name words, action words, adjectives, adverbs, Alice built into her vocabulary. Thomas kept the children in spasms of laughter as he acted out the meaning of *sad, angry, fast, slow, tumble, fly* . . . He believed that laughter and happiness opened the doors to a child's mind, that gloom and force closed them.

The children and he went for walks, finger-spelling all the way. Alice ran from bush to tree to flower asking the names of things. At other times, she and his six-year-old brother, Edward, searched pages of print for words they had learned. Thomas deplored the fact that there were so few, practically no books for children. Some

day he promised himself he would alter the situation—
he would write a whole library of books for boys and
girls. For the present he reduced stories to the fewest
and simplest words. Alice was as excited as a schoolgirl
over her first report card when she could read a whole
story.

Thomas received his degree from Andover College
on September 23, 1814. Immediately after graduation
he began his plan of "preaching occasionally and travel-
ing considerably," searching out the deaf—children,
youth, and grown-ups—of Connecticut.

Not all of the deaf were like happy, emotionally-
healthy Alice. One mother reported that her small son
at times acted like an animal gone mad. When he saw
the family talking together, he would make his lips move
in imitation of theirs, but getting no results, would fly
at them scratching their mouths.

Thomas explained that all would be changed when the
boy found a way of making himself understood; that it
would take time and patience to get across the idea that
things had names, but after the first word, progress
would be more rapid.

Thomas's diary doesn't say how far he traveled, nor
how many deaf he contacted, nor how many sermons he
preached, but references he made in letters to friends
indicate he accomplished all three.

Thomas was not the only one who had been active in behalf of the deaf. In April he received a note from Dr. Cogswell requesting that he meet with a group of Hartford citizens in his home on Thursday, the thirteenth. The men were meeting to give study to the idea of establishing a school in Hartford for the deaf of New England. There were those in the group who were doubtful of the ability of the deaf to learn. Would Thomas meet with them and tell his experience teaching Alice and others?

Thomas met with the committee. He spoke earnestly of the great possibilities for those handicapped by deafness if education were made available. His words carried the conviction of experience. Dr. Cogswell quoted statistics as to numbers, and told of the schools for the deaf in Europe; that America had none.

The committee was convinced that America should not lag behind in any field of service, that there should be a school for the deaf, that Connecticut should lead the way. It was voted that if funds could be raised, a young man should be sent to England to learn the oral method of teaching the deaf, and on his return he would help raise further funds and establish a school in Hartford. Thomas was surprised when Dr. Cogswell reported that the necessary funds had been raised in one day. He was still more surprised to learn that the committee was unanimous in its vote that he, "the young minister who spoke to them so convincingly on his work for the deaf," was the man who should be sent to England. Thomas had never thought of himself as that man. After all he had studied to be a minister and planned to fill a pulpit if and when his health permitted. He asked for a week to think it over.

During the week Thomas heard of a deaf-blind girl in Glastonbury, ten miles from Hartford. He wanted to see her and urged Dr. Cogswell to go with him to make the visit. The doctor consented and drove his team of grays. The girl was eight-year-old Julia Brace.

Mrs. Brace bade the visitors come in. She listened with interest as they told of the proposed new school for the deaf. As to teaching the deaf-blind she was skeptical, her skepticism based on her experience with Julia. Yes, she would gladly tell them Julia's story.

At the age of four Julia had been very ill with typhus fever which left her totally blind and deaf. She had gradually forgotten the words she knew, all except some words she should have forgotten and hadn't. Mrs. Brace shook her head. "Our Julia swears terribly, and throws herself around like one possessed when she gets angry. We know not where she learned the words unless from the sea captain who used to fish in our creek." She hastened to add, "We are Godfearing Meeting House folk, ourselves.

"Julia is most contented," her mother continued, "when she is helping. She brings in chips in her basket, and sets the table. Her greatest pleasure is 'seeing' new things and showing them to her sister."

Dr. Cogswell told Mrs. Brace that he had a little deaf girl only a year older than hers, and that he and Thomas would like to meet Julia.

Julia's sister led her into the room. After shaking the small limp hand, the doctor and Thomas took their watches from their pockets and placed them in Julia's hands to entertain her. The hands eagerly came alive. As each watch was received she rubbed the hand of the owner and then put her hand to her nose to remember him by smell.

Sitting on a low bench with her sister, she moved her fingertips very gently over each watch, smelled it, and then rubbed it against her upper lip where she apparently got a keener sense of feel. After satisfying her own curiosity, she directed her sister through the same routine of touching, smelling, and lip-smoothing she had enjoyed, but never letting go of the watches. She was then ready to return them.

Thomas and Dr. Cogswell exchanged chairs and tried to take from her each other's watch, but she would not allow it. She smelled their hands and returned each watch to its rightful owner, then quietly again took her place on the bench.

It was hard to imagine that this child of apparent angelic disposition could be guilty of the tantrums her mother described. But before the men left, they saw the angel turn into a small demon. It was over something she couldn't make her sister understand. After repeating certain awkward gestures over and over without getting her meaning across, Julia threw herself on the floor, kicking, screaming, and biting if anyone came near, while out of her mouth came a volley of the vilest oaths the men had ever heard.

How, Thomas wondered, could this child be released from the dark, silent dungeon of which she was frantically trying to beat down the walls. "I am convinced," he wrote in his diary later, "that it is the will of Heaven that not one of these little ones should perish." But he knew that Heaven was depending on humans to carry out its purpose.

Each day the conviction grew that he should say yes to the committee's proposal. Both his mind and his heart told him he had found the work meant for him. His health problem seemed to step aside as if saying, "I will no longer interfere." At the end of the week's grace he wrote his reply to the committee.

The same evening on the first page of a brand new diary he wrote:

> *Hartford, Conn., Thursday Evening, April 20, 1815. Today, I informed Dr. Mason F. Cogswell ... of my willingness to undertake the employment of instructing the deaf and dumb in my own country.*

CHAPTER 5

England—Scotland

THOMAS stood at the rail of the small sailing ship *Mexico*, as its wake lengthened the distance from the New York wharf. He waved to his family—Peter Wallace, his father, had recently moved the family to New York—until they blurred into the background of city buildings.

In his pocket was his passport to England, signed by Secretary of State James Monroe. It described him as "5 ft. 6½ in., darkish complexion, dark gray eyes, thin in person . . . straight nose, full lips . . ."

How long would it be until he again saw the shore line that was gradually receding from sight? Less than a year, he hoped. With fair sailing the voyage over would consume a month, the same on return. While in England

58

he would study as he had never studied before. Based on his experience of teaching Alice and his contact with other deaf children and adults, he was confident he could master the professional methods of instructing the deaf within three months, at the most six. Yes, well within a year's time he should be back in Hartford, raising the final funds necessary to establish the school for the deaf. He thrilled to his very fingertips with enthusiasm.

Misty haze finally claimed the last church steeple of New York. The escort of sea gulls, supposedly calling *bon voyage*, but most likely shrieking threats against the ship for not producing more handouts, began to thin. Thomas turned to his cabin and settled himself for the next four weeks. Taking the new diary from his valise he wrote:

May 25, 1815—Today I sailed on the ship Mexico bound for Liverpool, England. May the all-wise Father bring us safely to our desired haven.

The *Mexico*, being a light ship, burden three hundred tons, chose to ride the ocean swells rather than plow through them. Thomas was thankful that he seemed to be equipped with a pair of conditioned sea legs. He walked the deck with Washington Irving who was on his second voyage to England and Scotland. They walked miles discussing a common interest, literature and writing. Thomas spent hours studying French and reading the *Théorie des Signes*, the Abbé Sicard's book of signs and finger-spelling which he had brought along with him.

He was interested in learning the origin of the French system as described in the book. It began, so the author said, with the Abbé de l'Epée (1712-1789). As the abbé walked down a certain street of Paris, calling on the members of his new parish, he stopped at a home where, through the open door, he saw two girls busily sewing. He was surprised when they did not answer his knock or pay any attention when he spoke to them.

The mother coming home just then informed him with tears that the twins' seeming rudeness was because they did not hear his knock or what he said, that they were both deaf-mutes. "We are desolate," she said, "and know not what to do." She explained that a priest, neighbor to them, had been trying to teach the twins about God and heaven, right and wrong, by means of pictures, but the priest had died. "What will become of my girls?" she asked. "Must they perish for lack of knowledge?"

Abbé de l'Epée assured her he would do what he could to instruct the girls in religious matters. He used pictures and gestures, acting out what he wished to teach since he had no other means of conversing with them. He was so successful that soon other deaf pupils joined his class.

Strangers who visited the class offered him a book they had to sell, a book telling of a way to converse with the deaf. At first the abbé refused to buy the book because it was written in Spanish, but on learning it was a manual of signs and finger-spelling written by the Spanish teacher of deaf-mutes, Juan Pablo Bonet, he purchased it, and set himself the task of learning Spanish that he might read it. He revised the book to fit French customs and used it as a guide in his teaching. His pupils learned to finger-spell and to sign, and by this means to converse. The class grew until it became the well-known Royal Institution for the Deaf and Dumb, now headed by Abbé Sicard, who again revised the book, the edition of *Théorie des Signes* that Thomas was now studying.

Thoughtfully, Thomas closed the volume. In a way wasn't he a sort of Abbé de l'Epée, learning a language to acquaint himself with signs and finger-spelling, and then establishing a school for the deaf? Would he also revise the book? It was his plan to study both systems of teaching the deaf—the English oral method by which the deaf learned to speak artificially with the voice, and the French manual method by which they spoke with signs and finger-spelling. He hoped to combine the best in each system when establishing the school in America.

The *Mexico* docked at 3 P.M. on June 25, at the Liverpool wharf. So far his schedule was holding. It had been one month to the day since he sailed from New York.

Thomas walked confidently through the streets of London to the address of the chairman of the Committee of the Asylum for the Deaf and Dumb. The buildings on both sides of the narrow streets were so tall they seemed to lean together shutting out the sky. Thomas didn't recognize this as an omen that other things besides sky might be shut away from him.

The Committee was willing to help him but he found the instructors of the deaf did not cooperate with the Committee. They had not only closed the door to their methods of oral instruction, but locked it as well.

There were many private schools in England; for fifty years the education of the deaf in the country had been under the monopoly of one family; a monopoly that had profited handsomely; a monopoly so strong that schools in Ireland had been prohibited. And at that very time a member of the family was in America trying to extend the monopoly to Thomas's own country. "Sad monopoly of the resources of charity," he wrote in his diary. Only deaf children with rich parents or relatives, and those few poor who were chosen and financed by Subscribers—well-to-do Englishmen who were interested in the deaf—could hope for an education. On July 8, Thomas's diary tells of one of the "sorriest sights" he had ever seen. It was the day the Subscribers voted on the deaf children whose schooling they would finance during the year.

The Committee of the Asylum for the Deaf and Dumb had advertised it would receive applications in the second floor ballroom. Early in the morning the stairway leading to the ballroom was lined with shabbily dressed parents and their scantily dressed deaf children. As the Subscribers in velvet cloaks and ruffles passed up the stairs, the parents presented their handicapped children, together with tickets which gave the account of their circumstances and claim on charity. Out of the seventy-three children on the stairs, sixteen were chosen.

Revulsion at such a practice welled up in Thomas like a knot. He clenched his fists. Every child in America should have a chance. And then he relaxed. He needn't worry. The benefactors at home were planning such a program.

Thomas was thrilled when he learned that Abbé Sicard was in London, with two of his young deaf instructors, giving a series of lectures and demonstrations on the French system of teaching the deaf. He would meet the author of the book he was studying! Newspapers reported the lectures were creating city-wide interest. Ladies and gentlemen of nobility were attending.

The next lecture would be at two o'clock that afternoon. Thomas made it a point to be early. The abbé was very old, a small thin man, but with a wit as sharp as his nose. The climax of the afternoon came when he introduced his deaf assistants, blond teacher Jean Massieu and swarthy teacher-printer Laurent Clerc. He invited the audience to ask questions that would test the young men's education. The abbé translated from spoken to sign language. The young men wrote their answers on a blackboard. The result was a double contest, the audience trying to out-do one another in asking difficult questions as well as testing the young teachers. Thomas noticed a scar on Laurent Clerc's left cheek that deepened when he smiled. He wondered what accident could have caused it.

After the lecture Thomas introduced himself to the abbé and his assistants, and told them the purpose of his visit abroad.

"You must visit the Royal Institution for the Deaf and Dumb in Paris before you return to America," urged Abbé Sicard, interpreting the conversation in sign language to the young men.

"The door will be open for you," spelled Jean Massieu on his fingers.

"Very wide," added Laurent Clerc and smiled. Again Thomas noticed the scar.

At the moment, Thomas thought a wide open door would be about the most beautiful thing in the world. Again and again he met with the Committee, with sub-committees, and the headmaster of the school for the deaf, but the monopoly family blocked his way. He was welcomed to demonstrations of the result of oral instruction, but not the methods. He heard deaf children speak with varying degrees of voice quality, from guttural tones to the more natural, as they answered questions which they read by watching the lip movements of their teachers. These pupils, before admission to the school, had been obliged to sign papers pledging themselves to secrecy as to the training methods.

Finally it was decided that if Thomas would sign a contract as a regular apprentice teacher for three years —the headmaster intimated it might take four or five

—he would be extended the privilege of learning, with salary. The hours would be from seven to eight and include supervision of the children's recreation.

Three years! Thomas had given himself three months! He could not accept the proposition.

He wrote Dr. Cogswell of his difficulty, also that the Committee had suggested he go to Scotland and visit the Edinburgh school. He might be more successful there. The extended trip would require more funds but he felt the men of Hartford would wish him to go. Since he could not expect a reply from them in less than two months, he had made the decision himself. He would be leaving London for Edinburgh the next week. It would be his last chance of learning the oral method of instruction in anything like a reasonable length of time.

"I long to see Hartford once more," he wrote, "and be in the midst of my deaf and dumb children. . . . I have not yet received a single letter from America. Tell Alice I shall hope to hear from her . . ."

Thomas boarded the smack, *Buecleuch*, and hopefully sailed the four hundred miles up the coast to Edinburgh. To his great disappointment he met the same monopoly. The headmaster of the school was most willing to help, but he had received his early training from a grandson of the monopoly-family, and had been obliged to bind himself to secrecy for seven years on bond of one thousand pounds. Four years had elapsed, three to go.

"Perhaps," suggested the headmaster, "if you wrote the family they would release me from my bond so far as America is concerned."

Thomas wrote. Titled friends, that he had made since coming abroad, wrote. Friends of the family wrote. But the monopoly was equally proof against stranger, titled rank, or personal friend. The answer was a positive refusal.

Thomas decided the only thing left for him to do, if he wanted to see a school for the deaf in operation, although not an oral school, was to visit Abbé Sicard's school in Paris. But he would have to wait until the political trouble of France had quieted, until the country had recovered from its recent revolution.

From August until February 1815, Thomas remained in Edinburgh. He preached in Scottish pulpits, attended a series of lectures on "The Human Brain," visited bookstores, purchased books for the new school, and studied French. One day he learned of a retired teacher of the deaf who was no longer under bond, and called to see him.

The man was old and gray. Yes, he would be pleased to help the young teacher from America. He invited Thomas into his study where they sat before an open fire, Thomas taking notes, the old teacher leaning back in his chair, eyes closed, reminiscing about the days when he taught the deaf.

"The first thing when teaching a deaf pupil to articulate with the voice," he explained, "is to get him vocalizing, first the vowel sounds, *ah, oh, ee* ... The consonants will come next. After he has learned these elements of speech, he is then taught how to put them together to make meaningful words." The instructor paused, Thomas turned a page in his notebook and waited.

"And now, how does he learn? With the fingertips he feels the vibrations of his teacher's vocal chords. He observes the position of tongue, teeth, and lips in producing speech. He imitates. A mirror will help him to compare his results with that of his teacher." There were many other suggestions which Thomas carefully recorded.

"Articulation requires a long period of training?" Thomas asked.

"A very long period. But the deaf child must learn speech that he may fit into a hearing world. He learns to understand what others say by watching the lip

68

movements of the speaker. Lipreading, it is called."

That evening, Thomas went back to his lodging feeling that even if he had not been privileged to observe in the classrooms of oral schools, his voyage to Scotland had not been in vain. In his diary he wrote of his visit to the retired teacher, adding that he had "procured much help."

A letter from Dr. Cogswell assured Thomas that the men of Hartford stood back of him both in the matter of money and his trip to Edinburgh, and if necessary to France. Enclosed with the letter was one from Alice. Dr. Cogswell wrote a note of explanation.

Alice's teacher, Miss Huntley (Thomas had urged the doctor to place Alice in Miss Huntley's Hartford school for girls during his absence), had told Alice in sign language about a Mr. Colt who was visiting the school. When Mr. Colt was a little boy, so the story went, he had long blond curly hair. A clergyman took a fancy to the curls for the purpose of making himself a wig. At first the mother refused but after much urging, "talk long" as Alice put it, she consented, the boy's hair was cut off, and the wig made.

"The letter is all her own," wrote Dr. Cogswell, "without assistance or correction. You know so much of her manner that I believe you will understand it."

Hartford, Wednesday, October 11, 1815
My dear Sir:—

I remember story Miss Huntley tell me. Old man Mr. Colt little boy . . . very much curls. Little boy hair Oh! very beautiful mama lap little boy comb curl love to see Oh! beautiful. Morning long man preacher coat black come bow ask mama give little boy hair make wig, mama no preacher yes talk long man say come back little boy scissors cut hair white curls all in heap make wig preacher am very much glad proud little—little boy head very cold mama tie handkerchief warm, tears no more mama very sorry. I hope my hair never cut make wigs—This morning study . . . very still very good noise no— the play no . . . come back little while—O all very glad—O beautiful—I love you very much—

Your affectionate
Alice Cogswell

Thomas thought back to the day not many months before when in the sand of the path he had taught Alice her first word. How far she had come! He would treasure the letter always. It was his first reward in his chosen work.

He wrote Alice, telling her how happy her letter had made him. He told her all about Scotland, especially about the school he had visited where deaf boys and girls learned to understand what people said by watching their lips. He suggested:

> *Look at people's lips when they speak. Get Mary and Elizabeth to speak some words to you, such as, chair, table, door, water, fire, run, walk ... and remember how their lips move ...*
>
> *I am glad you are studying hard. Help Miss Huntley. Love God.*
>
>

Your friend,
Thomas H. Gallaudet

CHAPTER 6

Open Doors and Open Arms

Paris, March 12.—Thomas made his way through the city's famed Market Place, through its Latin Quarter, and at last stood before the door of the Royal Institution for the Deaf and Dumb. He rapped the door knocker. The caretaker led him up the worn stone steps to Abbé Sicard's office.

When the abbé saw who stood on his threshold he flung the door wide, also his arms. He embraced Thomas, not once but many times, shook his hand, patted his shoulder, all the while repeating how honored he was that the young minister from America had come to visit his school.

"And now, my friend," said the abbé, offering Thomas a chair, "the Royal Institution for the Deaf

72

and Dumb awaits your pleasure. What can we do for you?"

Thomas, taken by surprise by the exuberant French greeting, collected his thoughts. "I have come, kind Father, to see how you operate so fine an institution, that when I go back to America I may be able to start a school for the deaf in my country."

"It is splendid! It is splendid, I repeat, that you have so worthy an ambition! When I was young I, myself, had such an ambition. Abbé de l'Epée taught me. Now, I, Abbé Sicard, will repay the favor by teaching you."

"How long do you consider that it will take?" asked Thomas. "I have already lost much time."

"That I cannot say. It depends on the learner." The abbé chuckled. "Cotton absorbs water faster than linen, you know."

Thomas was relieved to learn that he could set his own pace. He was sure that he could do even better than cotton when it came to absorbing ways and means of teaching his deaf pupils waiting for him at home.

"You will have class with me thrice a week," said the abbé. "Every day you will meet with my assistant, Monsieur Jean Massieu. Beginning with the youngest class you may observe the methods of teaching, and advance class by class until you reach the highest class taught by Monsieur Laurent Clerc."

75

"Monsieur Laurent Clerc?" asked Thomas. "Is he not one of the young men who accompanied you to England, the young man with the scar?"

"Ah yes," said the abbé, "a most excellent student and teacher. He was seven years a student and now eight years a teacher. Since you mention the scar I will tell you how he came by it. When an infant of one year he was left alone on a chair by the fireplace. Wiggling as the little ones do, he fell off the chair into the hot ashes. From that day his parents claim he has had no sense of smell or hearing."

Thomas shook his head. "I suppose everything was done for the boy that could be done?"

"It seems so. When he was seven his father took him to a doctor in Lyons to receive injections of some fluid twice a day for a fortnight." The abbé shrugged. "Science has no cure for deafness. Good people only waste their money and time trying to find one—"

"And he has lived here since," interrupted Thomas, wishing to keep the abbé on the story.

"No, he spent his childhood at home helping with the farm tasks—driving the cows to pasture, herding the turkeys in the field, leading his father's horse to water. It was when he was twelve that his uncle brought him here to the Royal Institution for the Deaf and Dumb. Jean Massieu was his first teacher."

76

"Has Monsieur Clerc learned the oral way of speaking?" asked Thomas hopefully.

"At one time he had the ambition to learn," said the abbé. "He took lessons outside of school hours, and learned to articulate all the letters of the alphabet and many words of one, two, and three syllables. But he had special difficulty with the sounds *da* and *ta*, *de* and *te*, also *do* and *to*. His teacher, becoming impatient, hit him a violent blow under the chin that made the boy bite his tongue. He has never tried to speak since."

The abbé paused. "Tch, tch, how shameful! A teacher must always be patient." Another pause. "Yes, my friend, that is the first lesson for a teacher to learn—patience, much patience."

Arrangements for classwork completed, Thomas stood up. The abbé embraced him again. "May your visit prove to be all you hoped for."

Thomas looked out of the small window of the French hostel. The sun shone down on a city of spires, belfries, and tall gray buildings. That very sun, he told himself, will be looking down on Hartford a few hours from now. The thought made him feel less a stranger, a little closer to home.

He would lunch at one of the small sidewalk cafés, but there was something he wanted to read first. Taking the second volume of *Théorie des Signes* from his valise, he pulled the only chair the room afforded, a straight back one, nearer to the window. Now that he had become acquainted with Laurent Clerc through the silver-haired abbé, he wished to know better the third member of the teaching trio, the one who would be instructing him daily, Jean Massieu. In the back of this second volume, he remembered, was a life story of the teacher, his own account, as quoted by Abbé Sicard. Thomas had read it sketchily before, now he read carefully.

> *Jean Massieu was one of a family of six children, all deaf-mutes. Until he was thirteen years and nine months old, Jean remained at home without instruction. He communicated by means of gestures with his parents and brothers and sisters, but complained bitterly that strangers could not understand him.*
>
> *When he saw other children going to school and learning to read and write, he went to his father with a book in his hands, and demanded to be sent to school like other children. His father tried to make him understand that he could not go to school because he was deaf.*
>
> *"At that I cried very hard," said Jean. "I put my*

fingers into my ears, and demanded that my father cure them. My father explained that he could not."

Without telling his parents, Jean slipped out of the house and went to school. He presented himself to the teacher, and by gestures asked to be taught to read and write. The teacher refused him harshly and drove him away from the school. This made him weep again. At home, he tried desperately to trace shapes of letters with a pen, but they told him nothing.

A neighbor spoke of him to Sicard, who was teaching the school for the deaf at Bordeaux at the time. Sicard wrote to Jean's father and offered to teach his promising son.

So he traveled with his father to Bordeaux where he stayed for three and a half years, and then transferred with Sicard when he was sent to the school at Paris.

"I found the abbé very skinny," said the boy.

Thomas laughed, and closed the book. He, too, had found the abbé "very skinny" in size, but fat, very fat, in kindness. He wrote in his diary:

Here at length I may consider my work as beginning. May I be spared to see its successful accomplishment.

79

Two busy months slipped by. Until now, Thomas had found no time to be homesick. Weekdays had been crowded with intensive study and observation, social appearances, and a little sight-seeing on the side. Week ends he acted as temporary pastor to an English-speaking congregation, preaching in the Chapel of the Oratoire.

But this Monday morning he was impatient to be on his way home. The sudden longing was caused from having unexpectedly met two American friends the day before, Captain Hill of the *Mary Augusta*, soon to sail from Le Havre for New York, and a business acquaintance returning home on the same ship. Both had urged Thomas to sail with them. Sailing ships didn't sail on a set schedule. He didn't know when he would have another so favorable an opportunity.

He lingered in Laurent Clerc's classroom telling him of his dilemma. He could not accept the offer of passage because he was not yet sufficiently qualified to undertake starting a school on his own. Besides, the signs in the *Théorie des Signes* still had to be reworked to fit American customs. He needed counsel on that project. No, he definitely could not go. If only the ship would sail a few weeks later. Slowly he gathered up his notebooks and walked toward the door. Then he stopped and spun around facing Clerc. An idea had come to him.

"You know, if I could get a deaf assistant to go with me, I could accomplish it!"

Clerc's face lighted with the eagerness of pioneering in a new land, but his hands spelled, "I am sure there are many deaf-mutes who would be willing to go, mutes who understand English."

Thomas chose the message of the teacher's face rather than his hands. He smiled. "There is only one whom I would choose—Laurent Clerc."

"But I know very little English," protested Clerc.

"You could learn, but we must say no more without first speaking to Abbé Sicard. It would be presuming on friendship."

Thomas decided that putting everything into writing was the best way to handle the delicate situation. Would the abbé feel he had been double crossed? Would he feel like a shepherd who had taken a wounded animal into his fold, and then after caring for it until it was recovered, found the ungrateful beast had repaid the kindness by stealing a sheep? Or was the abbé so devoted to the interests of the deaf that he would be willing, even pleased, to extend the blessing he had developed in France to the New World? He wouldn't be the first Frenchman to give such service. General Lafayette had adopted the cause of the American Revolution.

81

It was a long letter that Thomas wrote. One of the paragraphs read:

My country is already under great obligation to you, Reverend Sir, for the very great kindness with which you have given me free access to the advantages of your important establishment, but how would those obligations be increased, could you consent to send Mr. Clerc with me, as an illustration of the wonders you have performed in redeeming the human mind from the darkness of ignorance . . .

The closing paragraph:

I have taken the liberty, Reverend Sir, of expressing my thoughts in writing. . . . Could you furnish me with your reply in the course of a day or two, I shall esteem it a great favor . . .

Your obedient servant,
Paris, May 21, 1816   *Thomas H. Gallaudet*

Each day Thomas hurried to his room hoping a favorable reply would be awaiting him. One, two, three days—no reply. The abbé must be displeased. He couldn't blame him. After all, he was past eighty and needed the strength of the youthful helpers he had trained. Two more days went by.

On the sixth day a sealed envelope in the abbé's handwriting was pushed under the door. Thomas's hand shook as he broke the seal. There was but a single sheet enclosed:

> *I replied this morning at nine o'clock to my dear pupil, Clerc, and I give my approbation, with some conditions which he will communicate to you. . . . I make with pleasure, the sacrifice that you have asked.*
>
>

ce 27 mai, 1816
L'Abbé Sicard
>

Thomas tried to re-read the short note, but it blurred too much. He looked out of the window at a nearby church steeple. It, too, blurred. "Thank you, thank you," he whispered.

Thomas drew up a contract with Laurent Clerc for services in America covering three years. A time limit was one of the "conditions" the abbé had referred to in his letter, the other if his mother were willing. (Clerc's father was dead.) He left for Lyons for the necessary permission and to bid his relatives farewell.

Thomas and he went together to receive the abbé's parting words and blessing. Together they went to Clerc's classroom to bid his students good-by. A favorite pupil, Polish Count Alexander de Machiortz, took hold of his teacher refusing to let him go. The Count was a strong youth. Clerc had to struggle to disentangle himself. Finally he threw the young man to the floor and made a hasty exit from his weeping pupils.

The *Mary Augusta* pulled away from Le Havre dock the afternoon of June 18 in a favorable breeze, every sail spread and rounded taut. The ship crowded sail and Thomas exulted; at this rate the crossing would take less than a month. Another lesson in patience awaited him.

Halfway across the Atlantic the ship battled terrific headwinds—winds that howled through the rigging as if a squadron of banshees had attacked. The gale was followed by a great calm with not a breeze stirring the humid sluggish air. The limp sails hung as moss dripping from cypress trees until the sailors furled them. For days the ship was becalmed, with only the dragging anchor to slow its drifting off course with the current. There followed more days of headwinds . . . more days of breathless calm.

Thomas and Clerc made the most of the lagging time.

Clerc learned to write English, and together they revised the book of signs. They made plans for their fund-collecting tour which would be their first effort towards establishing the school.

After fifty-two days at sea, the *Mary Augusta* docked the morning of August 9, in New York harbor. Thomas immediately took Clerc to John Street to meet his family. He saw a puzzled look steal over the French teacher's face as his father and mother greeted them. He smiled to himself. Clerc was learning a first difference in customs—the difference between a French and a Puritan welcome, the one like a stream dashing over rapids, the other a deep quiet pool.

From New York, Clerc was introduced to the plainer stagecoaches of America. Thomas arranged a stopover at New Haven to visit Yale College. President Dwight welcomed them, interestedly inquired about their work, and showed them the new Yale Medical College. Clerc was impressed, he would have liked to have stayed longer.

The next stop was journey's end—the Cogswell home on Prospect Street, Hartford. Alice was at school but was immediately sent for. She rushed in and threw her arms around Thomas in a joyous embrace. This was a greeting Clerc understood. He said afterward that the homesickness which had been crowding him instantly left when he saw the child's face, one of the most intelligent he had ever seen. This was why he was in America—to make other children's faces shine as did hers. He was eager to begin work.

CHAPTER 7

"A Rare and Radiant Maiden"

I T WAS seven o'clock on an October evening in Boston. Thomas's spirits soared as he and Clerc took their places on the platform of the public hall. The room was well filled. Tonight he would use all the strength of argument he had learned in law, coupled with the gentle persuasiveness of the ministry, to present the need of a school for the deaf in New England.

He knew that in the audience there were three types of listeners—the scoffers, the curious, and those seriously interested. Scoffers were loud in their derision that it would be a waste of tax money to try to educate the deaf and dumb, with special emphasis on the word "dumb." Even from pulpits had been hurled the challenge that if God ordained some people to live in silence, they should live in silence.

Thomas had the answer to the first group in the man by his side. Clerc, the first educated deaf man ever to walk the streets of America, would soon show them how wrong they were about wasting tax money. For the second group, Thomas read the example of the Master Teacher when he healed the man dumb from birth. He laid the responsibility of children handicapped by deafness on the hearts of his religious-minded audience by passing on to them the plea of the deaf twins' mother to Abbé de l'Epée: "Must they perish for lack of knowledge?"

A bat fluttered in and out of a window unnoticed as Thomas told Alice Cogswell's story, and what he had seen in England and France where educated deaf people were beginning to fill responsible positions. As proof he introduced his friend, Laurent Clerc, successful teacher and printer. If the audience would care to ask questions Mr. Clerc would be most happy to reply by writing on the large blackboard in the front of the room.

The half-hour that followed proved to be a friendly get-acquainted bout between the audience that could hear and the young man from France who could not. Thomas translated the questions into sign language.

88

"What is the meaning of gratitude?" asked one.

Without hesitation Clerc wrote in a bold artistic hand, "Gratitude is the memory of the heart." A ripple of pleased assent ran through the crowd.

"What is eternity?" asked another.

"Eternity," wrote Clerc, "is a day without yesterday or tomorrow."

A man in the front row asked, "What does it mean *to believe?*"

For answer Clerc made a diagram on the blackboard:

$$\text{to believe} \begin{cases} \text{I say } \textit{yes} \text{ with my mind} \\ \text{I say } \textit{yes} \text{ with my heart} \\ \text{I say } \textit{yes} \text{ with my mouth} \\ \text{I do not see it with my eyes} \end{cases}$$

Questions and answers followed each other in quick succession until Thomas announced, "One more question."

A gray-haired man arose. "I wish the young man would tell us what education has meant to him."

Clerc was thoughtful for a moment, and then bowing to his questioner, he wrote: "Before the Abbé Sicard I had a mind but it did not think. I had a heart but it did not feel."

The old man, still standing, posed a concluding question which was almost a statement, "You love the abbé very much?"

Clerc smiled. "Under his care I passed from the class of brutes to that of men; whence you may judge how much I love the Abbé Sicard."

The audience stood in appreciation of this testimony. They were ready to come forward with gifts, both large and small, for the establishment of a school for the deaf in New England.

From Boston to Salem, New Haven, Albany, New York, Philadelphia, Burlington . . . seven months Thomas and Clerc went their fund-raising way, repeating the Boston performance, until the necessary seventeen thousand dollars were raised. They made special efforts to interview parents of deaf children, and to meet prospective students. At New Haven, Miner Fowler, a farmer from Guilford, brought deaf-mute Sophia, his nineteen-year-old daughter to meet the teachers. When Thomas shook hands with vivacious, black-haired Sophia he was certain that here was a girl who would excel if given a chance.

He visited the Fowler farmstead, and thought what wonderful surroundings in which to grow up—sea-washed air, fertile fields, and giant elms shading salt box houses. Violets bloomed in the meadows reflecting the sky, cowslips yellowed the marshes, wild roses outlined the lanes . . . but all this generosity of nature could not compensate for the loss of hearing of the two girls, Sophia and her older deaf-mute sister, Parnell, who, because they could not hear, could not speak, and were accounted dumb.

Thomas sat in the parlor and talked with the parents about their daughters' future. He asked what the girls knew about reading, ciphering, and the Bible.

Miner Fowler shook his head. "Nothing, nothing at all."

"They bake bread and churn," said the mother, "and do all the household tasks, including spinning, but that is all."

Sophia brought in a pitcher of cold cider and a plate of crumpets for her parents and guest. In answer to the question in her eyes her father explained by gestures that she would go away to school, and the gentleman who had come to visit would teach her to read and write and cipher. Laughing, she stretched her arms wide and shook her head as if to say, "All that? I never could!" But Thomas saw a burning eagerness to try, in the dark eyes.

That night the names Sophia and Parnell Fowler were added to Thomas's growing student list. After Sophia's name he wrote, "a rare and radiant maiden." He also added that she was a child-woman in intellect, who conversed with her parents and sister by primitive crude gestures, not knowing a single word of language; that she had no idea there were continents beyond the sea, or rivers other than the one that flowed near her home. She knew nothing of books, social customs, or of a God in Heaven.

On Wednesday, April 15, 1817, The American School for the Deaf, originally called The American Asylum, at Hartford, for the Deaf and Dumb, opened its doors to students. The doors were those of a rented building on Prospect Street. Here the students would live and have their classes, but at mealtime they would march single file across the street to the sunny dining room of the City Hotel.

The first student to enroll was Alice Cogswell. Six others arrived that first day, ranging in age from ten to forty, a bewildered half dozen. Away from their families who understood their self-made gestures they had no means of conversing. Without exception their troubled faces showed symptoms of homesickness. Alice flitted from one to the other, like a winged fairy, trying to make them feel at home. She was especially solicitous of the youngest pupil, ten-year-old George Loring from

Boston, who was not only deaf but blind in one eye.

Thomas knew that interesting activity was the answer to homesickness. He and Clerc immediately organized the students into classes. He wondered—when he had time to wonder—what he would have done without Clerc. His French assistant had been through such an experience before, first as student and then as teacher. He knew just what to do.

More students arrived the following week, some of them Thomas had taught before going to England, others he had met during his and Clerc's tour. Sophia Fowler was the fifteenth to enroll, Parnell, the sixteenth.

The enrollment climbed to thirty-three before the year was over. It was necessary to train an assistant teacher. Clerc informed Thomas that he found the American students every bit as apt at learning as the French; in fact, they had to be held back instead of being pushed. One that went ahead from class to class was Sophia Fowler.

The new school aroused great curiosity and drew many visitors. The most prominent visitor of the year was President James Monroe. A platform was set up on Prospect Street in front of the school and decorated with bunting. Flags that boasted fifteen stars and fifteen stripes rippled from standards. All Hartford gathered to hear America's first citizen. The President arrived by carriage and was escorted to the platform where he shook hands with the students who stood around its base.

After the scholarly address, Thomas, as he often did with guest speakers, invited the President to ask Mr. Clerc a question which he in turn would answer by writing on the blackboard before the assembly.

President Monroe squirmed in his chair, crossed and uncrossed his legs. Clerc stood ready for the difficult question. Again the President crossed and uncrossed his legs. He leaned toward Thomas. "Ask him how old he is." Everyone, including the President, laughed.

It was during the afternoon that the sign for president was invented—the sign of the tricorn hat. (President Monroe, in honor of the visit, had worn his three-cornered cocked hat.) Hands placed, half open, at the center of the forehead were firmly closed as they pushed quickly outward in a V-shape. No one knew which of the thirty-three students made up the sign, but soon all were using it as a title of deference to the fifth president of the United States.

The school year ended in June, and the students went home for a two months' vacation. Sophia wrote that Parnell and her father and she had arrived safely at

Guilford. Thomas was so pleased with the well-written note that he replied immediately:

> *My Dear Friend:—Today I received your kind letter. I read it with great pleasure. It was composed very well. I understood it all. I am very glad your father and you and Parnell arrived home in good health. I am glad your friends are well.*

(Thomas then described his boat trip to New York.)

> *I have been very busy buying books and pictures for the [school]. Alice [Cogswell] will be here probably tomorrow. I will show her your letter; how glad she will be to see it! I had a letter today from Loring; he writes thus: "I love very Miss Sophia Fowler."... When Mr. Clerc comes to your home give him my best [regards]. Tell him I have already written him two long letters. I hope he will stay and see you some days. I wish I could be at your home also ...*
>
> *I shall soon see you again. Next year we will learn more, and I hope love God more ...*
>
> *My father's family, especially my sister Ann, send their best regards to you and your sister.*
>
> > *I am your sincere friend,*
> > > *T. H. Gallaudet.*

Eleven months since Sophia had learned to read her first word! Thomas counted the words in his letter to her—two hundred and nineteen different words, and he knew she would read the letter without difficulty. He had been correct in his estimate of this student from Guilford.

Three years slipped by. Just when a strange indescribable feeling began to stir within him, Thomas couldn't say. Perhaps it was gradual. But when Sophia enrolled for her fourth year, 1820-'21, he thought best that she should not be in any of his classes. He would let no one know of this upsetting emotion. He was her teacher and she his pupil, eleven years younger than he. He would lose himself in the business of building the new school.

He took the blueprints from his desk and went over the drawing, detail by detail. The school was being built on the former Scarborough property, a seven-acre plot half a mile from the center of the city. It was three stories high and faced south. Best of all, there would be a fine workshop where cabinet-making and shoe-making would be taught. The dedication services were set for May 22, 1821.

Fall gave way to winter, and winter to spring, but the "strange indescribable feeling" had not left him. On the contrary it had grown. He decided he would conceal it no longer. He would find a secluded place like the sugar maple or Charter Oak and write Sophia a note telling her of the secret he had kept hidden.

The writing wasn't easy. He had written debates, college theses, sermons, and editorials. He had written letters to senators and presidents. He had even written to Sophia, but this letter was different. It would be the first time he had ever written a proposal of marriage.

At last the note, longer than he had intended, was finished. He sealed it with sealing wax and a prayer, and sent it to the "rare and radiant maiden" as he had termed her in his student list four years before.

As Thomas expected, Sophia was surprised. She pleaded her lack of qualifications for such a change in position, from farm-girl-student to wife of the school principal; that her education was just begun.

Thomas assured her that travel and meeting people would, before long, make her feel at home in society. "As to education," his eyes twinkled, "you would have the advantage of a private tutor."

Sophia and Thomas were married August 29, 1821. They took the stagecoach to fashionable Saratoga Springs, New York, for their honeymoon. When Thomas learned that Sophia had kept all his letters during the past four years, and had tied them with a pink ribbon "forever and always," he wasn't so sure that he hadn't been the dumb one when it came to matters of love. As they walked alone, his arm slipped about her, even as the pink ribbon around the letters, "forever and always."

They roomed in the elite Union Hall, drank "the waters" of the spring, climbed the Adirondack foothills, and took a hack to the Saratoga Battlefield, twelve miles distant. There, Sophia enjoyed a history lesson by her "private tutor" on one of the decisive battles of the American Revolution.

Thomas was proud of his bride as they sat on the hotel veranda and conversed in sign language. She was so graceful and queenly in a sparkling vivacious way.

There were always a few people who stared rudely, and another few, pityingly—he supposed there always would be those poor ignorant souls—but the greater part of the hotel guests accepted Sophia quite naturally. They wanted to meet the bride. Thomas was prepared to enlarge on her conversation, as he translated but found it unnecessary. He was amazed that she, who had been a stranger to language four years ago, could now manage the subtle turn of a joke.

If the honeymoon forecasts the marriage, Thomas and Sophia Gallaudet could look forward to a near-perfect life together.

G—8

CHAPTER 8

New School—New Courage

THE school year, 1821-1822, marked a high point in Thomas's life. He began it with a new wife, a new school building, and a new courage! He and Sophia lived at Number 30, Asylum Street, a modest frame home, but there were trees and a garden. The WEL-COME of the doormat, woven on Sophia's loom, meant what it said.

The school's enrollment soon reached a hundred and twenty-eight, with five associate teachers. The one count against the year was the vacant chair on the staff, Clerc's chair. No, Clerc had not returned to France when the contract expired. Instead, he had married and adopted America as his country. He was now on a seven months' leave of absence to guide the Pennsylvania school through its first year. Thomas knew just a small fraction of how the Abbé Sicard must have felt when he loaned Clerc to America.

Thomas made a note to invite young George Loring to Sunday dinner. The boy fairly drooped with Clerc gone; the two had become close friends, always speaking French when together. George had learned the language so perfectly that he astonished Clerc's Parisian friends who came to visit. Next to Clerc, Sophia could cheer the lad. He had looked to her as to an older sister from the first year of the school, when he wrote, "I love very Miss Sophia Fowler."

This morning there was a beginning class to start, a new teacher would be there, observing. But first he must get Fisher Ames Spafford, a blond-haired boy from Buckport, Maine, anchored to some useful activity. It was Fisher's third year at school, and he had arrived only yesterday afternoon to start the new term, but already he seemed to have covered the school's seven acres. He was reported climbing the roof of the old barn, investigating the fenced-off well, tinkering with the new machines in the shop. Thomas chuckled. If liveliness were a sign of genius, then Fisher should one day graduate *cum laude*. The boy liked to draw and paint. He would set him busy lettering signs for the new classrooms.

Now for the beginners' class. Snatching his quill pen from its holder—pen was an excellent first word—he reached for the doorknob of his office door; a knock came from the other side. Guests had arrived who wished to spend a day observing the school in session. He took them with him to the beginners' class.

Seven students sat waiting; seven faces that registered almost as many emotions—shyness, eagerness, sullenness. One girl was crying, no doubt from homesickness. Thomas showed them the pen, dipped it in an inkwell and wrote with it, then drew a funny picture to make them laugh. He let them examine the pen and take turns making marks on a sheet of paper. When he placed the pen in the hand of the tearful girl he gave the hand an extra squeeze. She smiled up at him through her tears.

He laid the pen aside, and with the forefinger of his right hand pretended to write on the palm of his left. The pupils imitated him. They had learned the sign for pen. Next he taught them to finger-spell the word:

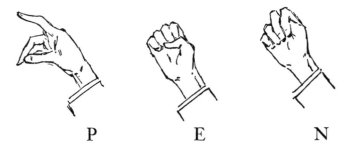

P   E   N

After the finger-spelling, Thomas wrote *pen* on the blackboard, and by gestures led the students to understand that those marks also meant the quill that could write. Eyes shone with the pride of possession and anticipation when the slates and slate pencils were given out. Such a scratching and squealing as slate wrote upon slate but the noise did not worry deaf ears.

"Not until a pupil can make the sign of the object," Thomas explained to the guests, "finger-spell it, and write it from memory on his slate, is a word considered learned. Each pupil may progress as fast as he is able."

Sometimes complications arose, as on this day. A boy produced a soft yellow goldfinch feather from his pocket, laid it on his slate, and proudly wrote the word *pen* beneath it. Thomas resorted to gestures to explain the difference between feathers and pens, that all feathers are not pens. He turned to the guests. "There is so much for them to learn, and so little time in which to learn it. Four years!" He shook his head. "Only four years the state allows."

Thomas introduced his visitors to other classes: grammar, geography, arithmetic, history . . . some of them he taught, others were taught by trained associate teachers. When a visitor raised a questioning eyebrow on seeing a teacher stop the class recitation to define such familiar words as *mountain, plow, plum,* or *president,* Thomas patiently explained that the deaf pupil is doubly handi-capped when he enters school. He must learn language which the hearing pupil has already acquired before entering school.

They visited the speech classes. Although Thomas had not been privileged to observe the methods of the oral schools, speech was taught at the American School from its beginning. No student who had learned to speak before becoming deaf, or who had partial hearing, was allowed to forget language, but was advanced by oral instruction.

Thomas took the guests on a tour of the shop. As the door opened they were met by the fresh pitchy smell of new wood and the stale brown smell of tanned leather. They examined a display of finished furniture, and then watched the process of shoe-making from the first cut of leather to the finished pair. Thomas proudly explained that orders were coming in faster than they could be filled.

The time of evening prayers Thomas reserved for himself. It was the part of the day he liked best. Then, the whole school family gathered together and he talked to them in both sign language and speech about God, the Father in Heaven. He marveled that he could never exhaust the subject. A hymn was sung in the language of signs. The music was the graceful rhythm of motion. Thomas believed that no one could know the depths of a song until he had sung it in sign language, for only then could it be felt by the whole being as it flowed from the heart to the fingertips. The Lord's Prayer, signed in unison, brought the vesper hour to a close.

The elm trees were again wearing spring green when Thomas opened his office door to a firmer than usual knock. A good-looking, powerfully built young man who would easily tower head and shoulders above any crowd, stood in the hall. He was red-headed and red-bearded. His gray eyes smiled as well as his broad mouth. Thomas shook hands with him and wondered if he would ever be able to sign and spell with that hand again.

The young fellow stooped from habit as he entered the doorway, and handed Thomas a note of introduction someone had written for him. From it Thomas learned that his visitor was Tom Brown, eighteen years old. He came from a farm in New Hampshire; he wished to learn to read and write, but most of all wanted to learn cabinet-making. Tom enlarged on the note with gestures of his own. He went through the motions of reading and writing, then measured a short span with his hands, indicating "a little would do." Shop work he represented by hammering and sawing, and stretched his muscular arms wide to show how much he hoped to learn in that field. Thomas looked at the huge hands, calloused from holding a plow in the furrow, and wondered how they could ever manage a pen or the fine finish of cabinet-making.

But time proved there was artistry in Tom Brown's hands. He ranked with the best in turning a spool bedpost or making a fine wood inlay. And when Thomas taught him the word *pen*, he wasn't satisfied with signing, finger-spelling, and writing the word, he wanted to know how to make the pen itself.

Thomas was pleased and took a class period to teach the art of pen-making. He taught his students how to dry the wing feathers of a goose in warm sand, told them that only the five strongest made good pens, and of those the left wing feathers were best because they curved outward from the writer. The right wing feathers might tickle the chin when writing. He led them through the process of scraping off the membrane, hardening the quill in boiling alum, and pointing it with a razor-sharp knife.

Thereafter, Tom made his own pens, and took pride in his writing. He wrote with a firm even hand, dotted his i's and crossed his t's carefully, but allowed his fancy to run in sweeping curves on the capitals. He made bookkeeping pens for Thomas from crow quills (crow quills wrote the finest lines). Presenting them, he signed, "The crows wish to pay for the peas they dig when you plant your garden."

Tom stayed two years after his graduation as assistant in the cabinetmaking shop. When he finally did go home (his aging parents needed him) he wrote Thomas he was now a different farmer from the one who had come to school. He read all the latest farm journals and farmed the "book way." To keep his "benefactors green in his memory," he had divided the one hundred and twenty-seven acre farm into lots of sugar brush, pasture, orchard, and woodland, and named them after his teachers—Gallaudet, Clerc, Peet, and Weld. Thomas hoped the sugar brush, assigned to him, had some implied meaning, such as sweet disposition.

The routine of weeks expanded into years. Thomas had not forgotten deaf-blind Julia Brace. He would never feel satisfied until a place had been made for her in the American School. When Julia's name was finally entered on the school roster, she had passed her eighteenth birthday. She learned to converse with the other students by placing her hand over theirs as they spelled manually. She learned to read an embossed primer by tracing the raised letters with her fingertips. Although she was very proud of her book and treasured it, she preferred doing useful work with her hands.

Julia made her own clothes and was keenly interested in styles. She was always pleased when a visitor, knowing her interest, invited her to "see" a new frock. Julia would go over the dress carefully with her fingers, noting details, and it was surprising how nearly she could duplicate it. Tucks or ruffles, bodice or bustle— she conquered them all. She seldom asked for help, not even to thread her needle, her tongue substituting for sight in the delicate task.

She still possessed her extraordinary sense of smell, and sorted the school children's clothes by scent even after they were laundered. She hemmed sheets and towels for the school, mended garments, and took care of the silverware. Thomas drew up a life-contract of employment for her with the American School. She enjoyed going on a visit to her Glastonbury home but always seemed happy to come back to her large circle of friends at her school home.

Observing the results at the Connecticut school for the deaf, other states became interested in establishing similar schools. They looked to the American School for teachers and teacher training.

One sultry August afternoon, Thomas saw a Kentuckian (couldn't mistake the hunting shirt) tie a tired horse to the hitching post in front of the school. The young man introduced himself as Adamson Jacobs from Danville, Kentucky. He had ridden horseback all the way to Hartford (reminded Thomas of his days as Yankee trader) to learn how to teach the deaf. It seemed his home town, Danville, wished to establish a school for deaf-mutes, and had hired young Jacobs as teacher. He was smart enough to know he needed special training and had set out to get it. After a stay of thirteen months he rode the same horse home again and established the Danville, Kentucky, school for the deaf.

The American School had now become parent to four such schools—the New York, Pennsylvania, Kentucky, and Ohio schools for the deaf. But the school was not alone in becoming a parent.

Thomas and Sophia had become parents, also. First there had been a boy whom Sophia insisted on naming Thomas. When the next baby was a girl with black hair, and eyes that promised to be brown, Thomas said there was no question but they had acquired another Sophia. The third they named Peter Wallace after Grandpa Gallaudet who was as active at seventy as a man half his age; he worked in the United States Treasury at Washington. The next baby was christened Jane in memory of Thomas's mother. There had always been a Jane in her family. And now there was small William who would be a year old day after next—five children, and all of them well and strong like their mother, but having the hearing of their father.

The increase in family, and increase of schools meant an increase in responsibility for the principal of the mother school. In his work, Thomas had reached a plateau only to see a new height before him. He cast about for the best way to attain this new height, this larger dream.

CHAPTER 9

April Again

THOMAS carefully wiped the quill pen with a scrap of cloth and placed it in its holder. He sealed the letter with a blob of red wax, snuffed out the candle, and put the stick of sealing wax in the center drawer of his office desk. Raising a window to let in the scent and sounds of April, he tipped back in the swivel chair and gave himself up to memories of the past, and plans for the future.

April, he mused, must be his decision month. It was on an April day, fifteen years ago, that his whole future was changed, the day the Hartford committee asked him to go to England to study methods for teaching the deaf. It was April when he first met Sophia; April, four years later, when he asked her to be his wife; April, when the American School opened its doors to students. And now, on April 6, 1830, he had made another important decision. He had just written, signed, and sealed his resignation as principal of the American School. Tomorrow he would hand it to the Board of Directors.

Why was he resigning? Did he feel that after fifteen years he had missed his life work? No, definitely not. He looked back now from the time of his graduation at Yale College, and saw that Providence had led all the way.

What he had considered misfortune, as different lines of work were blocked, was but a turn in the right direction. He had needed the knowledge of law as he stood before legislators and congressmen, needed a tutor's insight into students' lives, needed every principle he had learned in business as builder and manager of the American School, needed a minister's perspective to help students evaluate what is important and what unimportant.

Thomas ran his finger over the smooth cooled seal of the resignation letter. Then why was he resigning? There were three reasons. He had gone over them carefully many times:

First, the school needed reorganizing. It had started as a sort of family school, with principal, superintendent, and instructor having practically equal authority. Now that it had grown much larger there were too many heads, too many bosses. Too often it was "a house divided against itself." It needed centralized control with all departments cooperating. After a try or two towards bringing this about, Thomas saw that it would be easier to reorganize if he stepped out and a new principal took over. He had a man trained for the position. Lewis Weld, his former associate, now with the Pennsylvania school, could take over the mother school without a break in its progress.

Thomas had no intention of separating himself from the interests of the deaf. It was time, he felt, to expand that interest—time to start agitating the next step in their education—high school and eventually college training. Freed from the duties of school routine he would use his pen and voice towards this end. It would take time, perhaps many years. He might not live to see its accomplishment, but he could plant the idea.

A second reason for his resignation was equally divided between health and money problems. His health would not permit him to continue his present strenuous program: teaching six hours a day, keeping up with the growing correspondence, training new teachers, entertaining visitors, putting on programs before civic groups . . . He had asked to be relieved of the teaching, but the instructors had protested, not realizing to what limits they were pushing their principal.

He had never requested a raise in salary, and the directors seemed not to notice that many of the teachers received a higher salary than the principal. If he resigned he could see to it that the new school head began his work with proper authority, proper working hours, and a proper salary. This, he could ask for another but not for himself. Salary hadn't concerned him too much until his family reached the count of five. He must find a way better to provide for them, and he must plan for their education.

Thomas paralleled the resignation letter with the edge of his desk. The third reason for resigning made his pulse tingle with anticipation. He would be free to keep a promise he had made himself sixteen years ago, the promise that some day he would—

His office door hesitantly opened. "Mamma says to tell you that supper grows cold."

For a second Thomas was a boy again back in the kitchen on Prospect Street, smelling the baked beans and fresh rye bread, and hearing his mother say, "Have you been dreaming again, Thomas? Supper grows cold with the waiting."

Yes, he had been dreaming again—dreams that would

take years to fulfil. The swivel chair creaked to an upright position. "Coming, Tommy."

Taking a red and green striped candy sack from a drawer of his desk, he handed it to his eight-year-old son. "Here is some toffee a visitor left for you and Sophie, Peter Wallace, Jane and Willie. Maybe you'll have to eat Willie's share because Willie hasn't any teeth."

Thomas put the resignation letter in his inside coat pocket, and out of his mind. His time now belonged to Tommy and the family. The letter could wait until after supper and the children's good-night story.

Later, when the house had settled into its evening quiet, and he and Sophia sat alone in his study, he decided it was time to share the letter with her. He noticed she was patching a pair of overalls about the size of young William, now at the creeping stage. The patch was a deep blue against the faded cloth of the overalls. How like Sophia, he thought, filling the gaps of all their lives with something colorful and substantial. All their married years, and there had been nine of them, her warm encouragement had replaced his doubts and worries, making him continue to believe in himself when things went wrong.

Slowly he drew the letter from his pocket. Sophia knew of his plan to resign but what would she say now that the deed was done? He indicated to her that he wished to talk with her. She fastened her needle in the cloth and waited. As he signed and spelled the contents of the letter he watched her face. He anticipated an expression of worry, worry over the loss of a regular salary though that salary had been small.

Instead, Sophia thoughtfully looked up at the filled shelves of books and then at the vacant place on the wall beside them. She smiled as her fingers told him, "You will have to build more shelves. You will write many books."

Shelves! Books! Bless her, always a step ahead of him! The writing of books was the third reason for his resignation. Since the days when he had first taught Alice Cogswell, and discovered there were practically no books for children, he had promised himself that some day he would write books for girls and boys. True, he had written the texts used in the school's classes, this had been a necessity, but now he could write as Sophia said, "many books." Through his writing he could fill a need and at the same time better support his family.

The Board of Directors accepted his resignation only on the condition that he remain on the board as a general director and advisor of the school. This he was glad to do. As director he could carry forward his chosen work in a still stronger way. Clerc wept when his friend left the staff.

Lewis Weld became principal of the American School in October. The Board of Directors carried out Thomas's suggestions of centralized authority, a proper work load, and adequate salary. Many hours Principal Weld spent in his advisor's study discussing school problems. It became his second office.

Thomas sharpened a supply of quill pens (he wished for Tom Brown) and began writing books for children. Since he believed the Bible should be the center of education, and found some religious topics hard for them to understand, his first books were *The Child's Book on the Soul*, and *The Child's Book on Repentance*. After that a series of biographies on Bible characters from Adam to Jonah.

The mail brought Thomas many invitations to other positions; among them, he was invited to pioneer the work for the blind in Massachusetts; New York University offered him the chair of Philosophy of Education. The work for the blind tempted him, but he chose to remain in Hartford and write books. Hartford and the American School were next to his heart. When the town built a new jail he volunteered his services as chaplain.

The year 1830 hung black crepe on doors. First, his

brother Charles passed away, and then on December tenth, Thomas's birthday, a messenger from the Cogswell home brought word that the doctor had died of pneumonia after a five-day illness. Thomas and Sophia called at the Prospect Street residence to inquire if they could help the stricken family in any way. They were especially anxious about Alice. She and her father had been so close. But at the time of their visit Alice seemed the calmest in the household. She went quietly about among the visiting relatives helping those who were staying to get settled.

Later that night the Cogswell messenger knocked again. "Missus Cogswell say 'Please, Mister Gallaudet, come quick.' It is Missie Alice, she—" He was unable to explain.

Thomas could imagine his young friend unconsolable with grief; he was unprepared for the scene that met him at the Cogswell home. Alice had gone berserk, thrown her sister to the floor, and was wildly beyond control. At the firm clasp of her teacher's hand, the hand she respected next to her father's, she quieted down and allowed herself to be led to bed.

Thomas stood by her bedside and gained the attention of the wandering, delirious eyes by the sacred sign of the Wounded Hand. Gradually her reason returned. He talked to her about her father and what he would want of his Alice, until she became calm and promised to try to sleep. As he left, she smiled and signed, "Good night."

Dr. Cogswell was buried the next day. Thirteen days later Alice was buried beside him. She could not live without her father.

Thomas's pen continued to write. Besides the religious books he, with the Rev. Horace Hooker, compiled *The School and Family Dictionary*, and edited the *Practical Spelling Book*. He wrote articles for magazines on the need of teacher training and the supervision of elementary schools. Teachers of the deaf were trained in methods but teachers of the hearing taught very much as they pleased, setting their own standards which sometimes were no standards at all.

As a result of his writing and teaching experience, Thomas was invited to start a teacher-training department at Princeton University. Connecticut invited him to become the state's first Superintendent of Schools, but he preferred to let others have the laurels while he worked behind the scenes. He often traveled with Superintendent Henry Barnard, who was chosen to fill the position when he declined, helping him to organize the state's program of teaching.

Thomas and Sophia's family continued to grow. Two small daughters brought the family count up to seven.

First there was Catherine Fowler Gallaudet, and two years later, Alice Cogswell Gallaudet, named after that other Alice. Sophia's babies were always good babies. Perhaps it was because she did not hear them cry that they seldom cried. They learned to sign *mama* almost as soon as they could say *papa*. The small thumb brushed down the side of the face (from ear to chin), then swooped with both hands into the air as though rocking a cradle. One rock for mother, two for grandmother.

Thomas and Sophia remodeled a room of their home as a schoolroom and furnished it with desks and benches. They invited some of their friends' children to join their five of school age, and started a private school. A teacher was hired but Thomas himself heard their lessons once a week. The younger children were allowed only three hours of school a day. With slates and pencils they waited eagerly for their three hours to begin.

"Why can't we have more school, papa?" asked Jane.

"School is like the apple dumplings you enjoy so much. If you had them too often you would tire of them."

Jane didn't see how that could be but if papa said so it must be true.

Thomas often put aside his writing to go into the schoolroom to have a sing or to tell the children a story. One day he saw young Thomas skipping the serious parts of his book, reading only the story. He stooped and whispered, "You must read books like you eat pumpkin pie, eat the crust with the filling."

The pages of Willie's book were sadly bent at the corners. "Oh, oh," whispered Thomas, "your book is growing dogs' ears. Too bad, because dogs aren't allowed in school. You will have to stay home with it tomorrow."

Willie's face puckered. He liked school. Carefully, he straightened each corner, and carried the book to Thomas. "Look, papa, the dogs' ears are gone. Can me and my book come to school, tomorrow?"

"Of course," said Thomas, overlooking the *me*. Willie had had enough correction for one day.

Returns from Thomas's books began to come in. They were selling by the hundreds, in foreign countries as well as in America. *The Child's Book on the Soul* had been translated into French, German, Greek, Chinese, Siamese . . .

The Prince of Siam wrote:

> *City of Bangkok, Siam*
> *Sir: . . . I was brave to write you, asking you for some certain books . . . suitable to me for easily reading: every book of which you were author, and which were printed, and still remain some at your*

hand . . . I have now but one of books which you prepared. It is story of Joseph.

I hope very surely that you will be graceful to me, though I am your heathen, and was not acquainted with you at all. Please pardon me if I mistake by unproper word . . . as I am just learning this language, indeed.

The Prince T. Y. Chaufa Mong Kut.

Thomas and Sophia packed a bundle of all the books Thomas had written, including the speller and dictionary, and tied it with strong Connecticut hemp rope. Thomas knew the principal reason Prince Chaufa Mong Kut wanted the books was to learn the English language.

On the day the books were shipped he gathered the family together; they took hold of hands and kneeled around the bundle. Thomas prayed that the books would help the future king of Siam, not only to learn a new language but to learn of a new Friend who understands all languages and is a Friend of all people.

CHAPTER **10**

"Richer than You Think"

SUNDAY, February 5, 1837, was bitterly cold. Timbers of the Gallaudet house protested the weather with creakings and groanings. Icicles hung from the eaves and window frames outside. Frost had entered the inside by way of cracks around doors and windows outlining them with an etching of crystal white.

Thomas put another log on the fire. The fireplace seemed a cavernous monster that consumed quantities of fuel without much return in heat. He chose a long-burning hickory log, hoping the hickory had stored up an extra amount of summer sun. He then resumed his waiting which already seemed overlong. Only the two in the bedroom and he were in the house. The children were at the neighbor's. He kept an anxious ear turned toward the bedroom from which he was barred by propriety. And then he heard it—the cry of a newborn baby.

After a time the midwife appeared in the doorway. "You may come now, Mr. Gallaudet. You have a fine boy."

Thomas took Sophia's hand. His first concern was for her, and then his eyes sought the blanketed bundle in the cradle. "Shall we name him Edward?"

Sophia tiredly smiled assent. "And his middle name," she spelled, "shall be Miner, after my father."

"Edward Miner," said Thomas, gently rocking the cradle, "you have made our family complete, four girls and now four boys." A thought flashed through his mind, "And maybe you will complete your father's work." But Edward Miner slept soundly on, unmindful he had, or ever would make anything complete.

From the day Edward could walk, Thomas was shadowed by his youngest son. No matter that he was fifty-four and Edward four, he always had time for an inquiring boy; even when that boy crept into bed with him in the early morning hours and asked questions about bugs and stars, trains and triangles, and "where do the noises go, papa?"

There was the day Edward stood in the doorway, tears on his cheeks, and a dead rabbit in his arms.

Thomas pushed aside his writing. He was doing research for son Thomas's final thesis for Trinity College. The thesis was on their Huguenot ancestors at the time of their flight from France after the Revocation of Nantes, which took away their right to worship as they chose. But what was a past tragedy that couldn't now be helped as compared to a present four-year-old's that could. "We'll make the bunny a coffin," he said, "and have a splendid rabbit funeral."

During the next half hour the backyard echoed with the sound of sawing and hammering. Edward pounded in the last nail. "Where'll we bury him?"

"Why not bury him beside Alice's canary in the shade of the sugar maple?"

"Will you write a poem, papa, like you did for Alice's canary?"

"Of course," promised Thomas.

Up the hill under the sugar maple they dug a grave for the rabbit. And then while Edward picked spring beauties to place on the new mound, Thomas wrote a verse to read over it.

"Can we have another funeral," Edward asked on the way home, "when another rabbit dies?"

"I suppose so. But you don't want your rabbits to die, do you, Eddie?"

Edward shook his head. "N-n-o-o, but rabbit funerals *are* nice."

Thomas depended on his old friend Ventriloquist Granny to keep the younger children in line. They loved the charcoal-face, handkerchief-bonneted old lady he made out of his left hand. She knew so many wonderful bedtime stories, but might stop in the middle of one and, with her head bobbing and mouth clacking wide, say to a child, "Eddie, did I see you hide the crusts of your bread under the table ledge?" or "Catherine, did you remember to hang up your coat?"

Thomas seldom used the rod. The older boys would have preferred whippings, he knew, to talks in the study, but whippings only touched bodies while talks touched hearts.

Curfew in the Gallaudet home was eight o'clock. When one of the boys seemed to be forming the habit of coming in at ten, Thomas waited up for him. "Come," he said, "I have been wanting a partner for backgammon. Let us have a few games." He kept the sleepy boy playing the boring adult game until midnight. Nothing was said about curfew but the boy was in at eight o'clock the next night. He wouldn't risk another backgammon session.

The most severe punishment Thomas meted out was to Peter Wallace. Peter had put an old shoe in the deaf-mute seamstress' bed, making it look like a rat, and nearly frightening the woman out of her wits. Thomas sentenced the boy to his room for a week, except school hours, with nothing but bread and water. "The first lesson for everyone to learn," Thomas told him, "is respect for the rights of others."

Thomas often took one of the boys with him on short trips—to climb Mount Holyoke, to see Mr. Merriman, the dictionary-maker, or to attend some special program at the state capitol. Edward was five, and still wearing his hair in curls, when his father took him to see his brother Thomas march in the graduation parade of Trinity College. He held Edward's hand as the youngster balanced himself on the curb watching the band and the dark-robed figures march by. Suddenly one of the dark-robed figures stepped out of line and bent over the boy on the curb. "Eddie, don't you want to march in the procession?" Eddie did.

As Thomas saw his eldest and his youngest sons marching sedately hand in hand, eyes straight ahead, he was suddenly struck with the significance of the moment in relation to the future. Those two sons would join hands to carry the work their father had started to its completion, the work of educating the deaf. Thomas was so engrossed with the idea that he hardly heard

when a neighbor suggested, "Shall we go in and hear the orations?" and he found he was standing practically alone in the empty street.

Thomas had accepted the part-time position as chaplain of the Hartford Retreat for the Insane the year after Edward was born. He had been interested in the working of the mind since the lectures in Scotland. In the American School it had been the problem of helping minds, which till then were little used, to begin the process of thinking. Now he attempted to cure minds that were sick from having detoured from the road of sound thinking. He tried to lead them back to where they had detoured and help them to take the right road. In his diary he wrote:

I am becoming more and more convinced that a balanced physical and religious education on the simple principles of the Gospel, with early piety, constitutes the best security against mental (illness), and if it must come . . . will result in restoration.

Sometimes Thomas was obliged to think and act quickly in his work at the Retreat. Once, after entering a room and closing the door behind him, a maniac met him with uplifted knife. Thomas stood his ground.

Quickly taking a couple of keys from his pocket, he began twirling, tossing, and catching them. He smiled at the man. "I don't believe you can do this." The man traded his knife for the keys.

The women at the Retreat showed their appreciation of the chaplain by presenting him with a Scripture quilt. On the quilt they had embroidered numerous texts of Scripture. A verse written by a patient accompanied the gift:

> *These passages of Scripture truth*
> *You've made familiar from your youth;*
> *But each of us has placed them here,*
> *An emblem of our love sincere.*

The quilt eventually found its way to the boys' room. One morning Thomas questioned their report that they had read the required number of Bible verses. "How could you," he said, "when I find no Bible in your room?"

The boys answered in triumphant unison. "We read the Scripture quilt."

The Superintendent credited many of the cures at the Retreat to the patient, quiet, persistent work of the chaplain; but it was taxing work. Thomas lost weight. Sophia insisted that he "take the cars" (stagecoaches had given way to trains) and spend a few weeks at some northern lake. Thomas took her advice.

From the lake, he wrote that he had met an old sea captain he had known in Hartford. The captain had weighed him. "Already I've gained five pounds! I now tip the scales at one hundred and twenty-five." Enclosed with the family letter was one to Edward:

My Dear Son Edward:

How I want to see you and go out with you and look at your rabbits. Do they grow well? And what names do you give them? Do you help your dear mother all you can? . . .

                              From your affectionate Father
July 29, 1846

And now Thomas and Sophia were grandparents! Son Thomas who had married shortly after graduation, and gone to New York to work for the deaf, wired, "A fine girl [Caroline], all well." When two years later another telegram announced the arrival of Rose, Thomas insisted that it was Sophia's turn to take a trip; that she should spend Christmas with the grandchildren she was hankering to rock.

As they stood on the station platform waiting for the train, Thomas thought Sophia had never looked more beautiful than she did that day, wearing her new cape and bonnet, her brown eyes bright with the expectancy of the trip. He gave her a parcel he had carefully wrapped for granddaughter Caroline. A note was attached:

Dear Granddaughter:

Grandpa sends you a little book for a Christmas present. I send three kisses by grandma, one on the right cheek, one on the left, and one on the lips.

Be a good girl, love God, love to pray.

From your loving Grandpa

Thomas watched the train puff out of sight and thought what a lonely world it would be without Sophia. He walked slowly homeward to plan the next day's work at the Retreat, to help the children with home routine, and to complete an article on "Higher Education for the Deaf." Why did it take others so long to see what he saw so clearly?

Edward was twelve when Thomas decided it was time to talk to the boy about his future. It was strange, he mused, how children with the same parentage and the same training could choose so differently, when it came to professions, as did his and Sophia's eight. Their eldest, Thomas junior, was already recognized as an

136

authority on the work for the deaf as Rector of St. Anne's Church for Deaf-Mutes in New York; Sophia, a nurse; Peter Wallace had chosen to be a broker on Wall Street, New York; Jane, a teacher in the Hartford School for Girls; and William, an inventor. The two younger girls, Catherine and Alice were interested in home-making and music. Alice played the piano well.

It was in connection with the piano playing that the first incident as to their mother being different had entered the family circle so far as he knew. One evening when guests had complimented Alice on her piano solo, Sophia wistfully spelled that she wished she could have heard it. Alice had quickly left the room.

Thomas became suspicious when she did not return, excused himself, and went to find his daughter. He found her sobbing into her pillow.

"I'll never, never play again," she vowed. "It isn't fair to play music that dear mama doesn't hear." Alice sat up and wiped her eyes. "Oh papa, it's the first time I ever thought of mama being different."

Here was a problem that must be disposed of tactfully but firmly. The children must respect, not pity their mother.

"True, your mother does not take part in the music,

but doesn't she do everything else just as well or a little better than most folk?"

"Oh yes, I've heard guests from Europe say she is the most gracious hostess they've met in America."

"And that gracious hostess would be the most disappointed of anyone if her daughter did not go ahead with her music."

"But why, papa?"

"Because she knows what pleasure your music brings to you and to others. She is looking forward to the day when 'the deaf shall hear' and she will hear you play."

The light of understanding and determination came into Alice's eyes. "Papa, I'll work harder than ever on my music. I'll work up a program, the best program ever, to play on Mama's Hearing Day."

Yes, all of the family had settled on their vocations, all of them except Edward Miner. Thomas had taken it for granted that he would work for the deaf. The idea had been born with the boy, and reaffirmed on that Presentation Day at Trinity College. It was as if a voice had spoken.

Edward Miner returned a book he had borrowed from the study.

"Sit down, Eddie, let's have a chat."

Edward took the chair he had always sat in since he

was a little fellow and his short fat legs had stuck straight out from the chair cushion. Later, they dangled over the edge, and now they reached—in fact, over-reached—the floor. They sort of jackknifed at the knees.

Thomas closed the Bible, and put aside the material for his weekly sermon. Again he made an oft-repeated promise. "Eddie, when you want a Bible, I will give you one, a beautiful one."

Edward smiled, but shook his head. "Some day, papa."

"Have you thought much about your future, the profession you would like to follow?"

Edward squirmed to fit himself more comfortably into the lumpy chair. "Some," he said.

Thomas spoke of the work still to be accomplished for the deaf, their need for higher education, high school and college. He told of the joy and satisfaction he had found in beginning the work. He wondered if Edward wouldn't find the same in carrying on and enlarging it.

Edward sat up straight in his chair. His words, though not harsh, came like blows to Thomas. "But look, papa, you are a poor man. I'm going in for business or bank-ing, and build a fortune."

Thomas tried not to let his disappointment show too much. After all, a boy had a right to choose. Hadn't he, himself, at one time chosen business? "Go ahead, be a businessman if you must, but never a banker. A banker's work is too narrowing. What about college?"

"College isn't for me. I want to go to work right after high school."

There seemed nothing more to say. After all, his son was but a boy, maturity would probably change some of his ideas and values. Thomas stood up, so did Edward. He looked squarely into the clear blue eyes:

"There are other riches, my son, besides silver and gold. Perhaps some day you will decide that your father is richer than you think."

CHAPTER 11

"I Will Go to Sleep"

THE LEFFINGWELL house on Prospect Street where the Gallaudets had lived for the past eight years was sold. They had to move. Thomas combed the district near the Retreat but no rentals were available.

A house, valued at twenty-five hundred dollars, on Buckingham Street, was offered him for purchase. It was just such a home as he and Sophia had hoped some day to own. A flagstone walk led from the gate to the well-built house with honeysuckle shading its veranda. There was a grape arbor, a family-size orchard, and garden plot of rich soil. It was next door to an old friend, Seth Terry, with whom he had worked at the American School, and only a short walk from the Retreat. Thomas was beginning to feel the long walks he had been having to make. He would be sixty-three on his next birthday.

He took the small brown account book from his desk and studied it. The book showed a few dollars more than twenty-five hundred in their accumulated savings. They could buy the place, but should they? Should they put practically every dollar they had into property at his age, with his uncertain health and Sophia's handicap? His better judgment told him no, but there seemed nothing else to do.

Putting on his hat he decided to walk off his wavering uncertainty. Before he realized the direction he had taken, he was standing before the Buckingham Street house. Seth Terry joined him. "Decided to be my neighbor?"

"It appears so." Together they examined the tilth of the soil, discussed the pruning of the apple trees, and tested the well water.

"You were absent from the last directors' meeting," Seth reminded him, taking a folded paper from his inside coat pocket. "Chairman Williams sent you a copy of the business transacted. I said I'd be seeing you."

Thomas transferred the folded paper to his own coat pocket. "Thank you. That was very thoughtful of Chairman Williams and of you. Come to think of it, I don't remember receiving a notice of the meeting."

For once he didn't feel like discussing school business, his own was too pressing. He made a polite excuse and started home. A man ought to be in high spirits, he told himself, over the prospect of acquiring his own home, but under the circumstances he felt more depressed than jubilant. He was glad Sophia was out and he need not meet her questioning eyes and fingers.

After a brief nap he felt somewhat refreshed and decided to look over the directors' report. Unfolding the paper, he was struck with the long preamble. So many *whereases* must mean an important vote. He turned to the "voted" section on page two to see what it was all about. He couldn't believe what he read! He took off his glasses, wiped them with his pocket handkerchief, and then started at the beginning and read every word with care:

At a meeting of the Board of Directors held February 22d, 1850 Hon. Thos. S. Williams, president, in the chair, the following was, on motion of Seth Terry, Esq., unanimously adopted:

Whereas, *The Rev. Thomas H. Gallaudet has rendered many and great services for this institution, more particularly,*

Whereas, *Soon after he commenced his professional life, at the request of friends of the deaf and dumb he visited England, Scotland and France for the purpose of obtaining information as to the best mode of instructing deaf-mutes, and was absent on this business fifteen months; . . . and*

Whereas, *No pecuniary recompense beyond his actual expenses was ever made to him, therefore; and*

Whereas, *Since his connection with this institution as principal was dissolved, he has rendered valuable services for which he has not been compensated; therefore,*

Voted, *That we believe it to be the duty of this institution to make a reasonable compensation to Mr. Gallaudet for the time and labor thus devoted to this important work;*

Voted, *That the sum of two thousand dollars be appropriated for this purpose, and that the same be paid to him by the order of the directing committee on the treasurer, one-half payable on the 15th day of April, and one-half on the 15th day of July next.*

The report slid from Thomas's relaxed fingers to the floor. Minutes he sat staring out of the window, seeing nothing, enjoying the sensation of gratitude that tingled as it spread through his body. Footsteps in another part of the house brought him back to reality. He retrieved the report, and painstakingly copied it into his diary, adding:

In all this I see the hand of a kind Providence, locking up and reserving this sum for me till I most should need it; and when it would do me and my family the most good. O! Lord, lead me to be grateful and faithful. What shall I render thee for all thy benefits?

But this was not the end of the "benefits." On the day he received the deed to his house, he also received a purse of five hundred dollars sent by friends. He was so overcome that all he could say was, "May the Lord reward them." And thus it happened that when the Gallaudets moved on April 9, they not only had a comfortable home of their own but also a savings account that had not been touched in acquiring it.

The maples had begun to flame when William handed his father a thin, squarish envelope that had come in the day's post. Thomas examined the writing—a firm even hand with the i's and t's carefully dotted or crossed, and the capitals written with sweeping flourishes.

"Couldn't mistake that writing," he said. "Wonder what our friend, Tom Brown, has to say."

The letter proved to be an invitation to Thomas, Sophia, and family to a reunion of all Thomas's former deaf-mute students, to take place at the American School, September 26, 1850. Neither he nor Sophia could think of anything more to their liking. Eagerly, they counted the days.

At half past two on September twenty-sixth a procession formed at the American School and proceeded to Center Church. Leading it were three of the school's alumni—Tom Brown, as red-headed and red-bearded as ever, George Loring, and Fisher Ames Spafford. Then came the guests of honor—Thomas, Clerc, the governor of Connecticut, Lewis Weld, still principal of the American School, and the heads of other state schools for the deaf. The teachers were next in line, followed by two hundred former students, and the same number of Hartford citizens and friends.

On the platform of the church, sprays of autumn branches flanked a table on which were displayed two identical massive silver pitchers with silver salvers to match. The speakers took their places behind the table. The church, filled from floor to gallery, waited expectantly.

When the clock in the church steeple struck three, Principal Weld arose and welcomed homecomers and guests. Then Tom Brown stood up. In sign language, he said, "My spirit could find no rest until I had devised some method of giving expression to the grateful feeling in my heart which the years served only to increase. I had but to suggest the idea to my former associates when it was eagerly seized upon and made the common property of them all . . ."

The historian and orator of the day was Fisher Ames Spafford. Thomas smiled as in memory he saw behind the now dignified and kindly appearing superintendent of the Ohio School for the Deaf, a blond-haired boy climbing the roof of the old school barn. The liveliness had only needed harnessing. He was glad he had had a part in it. Son Thomas, Rector of St. Anne's Church for the Deaf, translated for the benefit of the hearing.

"Thirty-three years ago," began Fisher Spafford, "there were no educated deaf-mutes sent out into the world; now a large number. Who have been the instruments of this change? Messrs. Gallaudet and Clerc under the smiles of heaven. Our ignorance was like chaos, without light or hope. But through the blessing of God light shone through the chaos and reduced it to order. The deaf-mutes have long wished to express their gratitude to these benefactors . . ."

The applause was long and hearty. Names of other students were then called for impromptu speeches. A young man finally ended this part of the program by saying it would gratify him to address them but he found it quite impossible to collect himself for the purpose, for his thoughts were all in the silver pitchers displayed on the platform table.

This was the cue for George Loring, instructor in the American School for eighteen years, to play his role. George lifted one of the silver pitchers so that it caught a ray of muted sunlight from the multi-colored church window. A subdued gasp ran through the audience. He explained the cleverly etched engravings on the pitchers. On the one side, were pictured Thomas and Clerc in France looking across ocean waves toward America, on the other, the American School with teachers and students. A likeness of the Abbé Sicard had a prominent place between the scenes. On the necks of the pitchers were etched the different coats of arms of the New England states, and on the handles mute cupids forming the letter A of the manual alphabet. (The cost of the sets, three hundred dollars each, was reported raised with the "rapidity of a prairie fire" among the deaf alumni.)

148

George read the inscription of the pitcher he held in his hands:

Presented to
Rev. Thomas H. Gallaudet
First Principal of the American Asylum,
As a token of grateful respect,
By the deaf-mutes of New England.
Moved by compassion for the unfortunate
Deaf and Dumb
Of his country, he devoted himself to their
Welfare, and procured for them the
Blessings of Education
Hartford, Conn., Sept. 26th, 1850

Thomas went forward to acknowledge the tribute. For a moment, as he looked into the remembered faces, his voice failed. Composing himself, he addressed the alumni and guests in speech and sign language simultaneously:

"My former pupils and friends, I rejoice to meet you once more . . . Our separation has been long. Some of our number are no more—our beloved Alice Cogswell . . . We will ever cherish her memory.

"What should I have accomplished, if a kind Providence had not enabled me to bring back from France one whom we still rejoice to see among us—himself a deaf-mute—trained under the distinguished Sicard. . . . I beg you to accept my cordial thanks for the part with which you indulge me. I thank you all . . . In him, from whose hands I have just received the testimony of your grateful regard, I recognize one of my very earliest pupils, one whom I taught for a long course of years, and who now, in the maturity of manhood, is [teaching others]. This testimony of your affection I shall ever cherish . . . As I look at it from time to time, should my life be spared . . . I shall think of all the past in which you were concerned . . . with a father's love."

The presentation of the other silver set was made to Clerc. Following his reply, students, teachers, alumni, and the governor met in the dining room for a "bountiful repast" and social evening.

"What pleased you most, papa," asked Jane the next day, "the speeches, the silver set, or just meeting your old students?"

Thomas laughed. "Try again, daughter. The thing that pleased me most was neither speeches, silver, nor even the meeting of my students, although the latter, I admit, was a close tie. What pleased me most was to see the impression the group of educated deaf made on the visitors. Their intelligence, dignity, and courtesy prompted many a favorable comment." Thomas made a sweeping motion with his hands. "And this is but a sample of what might be if only high school and college were available to them."

July of the next year was extremely hot. Sophia insisted it was time that Thomas take his yearly vacation trip. But before he could get away they both took to their beds with a severe dysentery. Sophia's robust health soon had her up and about, Thomas was not so successful. He overcame the illness but seemed unable to regain his strength. He grew weaker day by day.

Regretfully, he dictated a note to the Convention of Instructors for the Deaf, that because of illness he would not be able to attend the August convention. He had waited until the last minute to send his regrets, hoping that he would be able to make it. The topic to be considered was one he had worked on for so long, "High School Education for the Deaf."

The secretary of the convention sent him a copy of the speaker's paper which ended with the dramatic appeal: "Who will undertake this enterprise? Our eyes involuntarily turn toward the vacant chair for the answer. But our father, our teacher, our guide lies ill upon his bed. Then who will undertake the work?"

Eagerly Thomas turned the page, hoping someone had volunteered. He sighed. No one had.

The same post that brought the report of the convention also brought a long slender parcel, evidently a mailing tube. He watched as Sophia carefully withdrew a parchment roll. It was a diploma, the honorary degree of Doctor of Laws, conferred on him by The Western Reserve College in Ohio for "recognition of his work as promoter of education in many forms."

"It has come just in time," Thomas said with a twinkle, "not to be too late." A friend who came to call, wrote his name as it would now appear—*Rev. Thomas Hopkins Gallaudet LL.D.* Thomas was pleased but not impressed.

On Monday, September 8, Judge Williams called and asked how he felt. "I hope I am better," Thomas spelled with his fingers.

Thursday noon he told daughter Sophia, who was fanning him, that he really did feel better. Taking her hand he turned himself over, saying, "I will go to sleep." Sophia continued to fan, and did not know until the doctor came and told her, that her father had gone to his eternal sleep.

There had been no final endearing words, no final admonitions to the family. There was no need. All through the years he had spoken endearing words, and admonishing words as needed. He had not left them until the last.

Funeral services were conducted by Doctor Harvey Prindle Peet and Laurent Clerc in South Congregational Church, Center Church being under repair. A host of mourners from all ranks of society followed the cortege to Cedar Hill to hear the final "Amen" to a good man's life.

The family returned home and found comfort in recalling the many good works of their father, and how those good works had returned to him, especially during the last seventeen months—owning his own home, the alumni memorial service, the LL.D. degree.

Edward remembered his father's words, "richer than you think," and understood. His thoughts troubled him and his conscience pricked as he watched his brother Thomas open the family Bible and record September 10, 1851 after their father's name. The sight of the familiar book reminded him of an oft repeated promise, "When you want a Bible, Eddie, I will give you one, a beautiful one." If only he had accepted the offer. If he only had.

CHAPTER **12**

His Father's Son

$\mathbf{A}$LL morning Edward Miner's thumbstall thwacked the crisp banknotes into piles of fifty; all afternoon he figured discount after tedious discount. He was well started in banking. He should have been thrilled. "I'm going in for business or banking and build a fortune," he had once boasted. "College isn't for me." But he wasn't thrilled. Now that college seemed denied him by the death of his father, it became his ambition.

"Too n-a-r-r-o-w-ing! Too n-a-r-r-o-w-ing!" The pendulous grandfather clock echoed his father's words with a measured, monotonous ticking. "Banking is too narrowing!" Edward felt the narrowing noose tighten month after month. He wanted to break its hold—expand his life—go to college.

Banking and college weren't the only things about which Edward had changed his mind. He now owned a Bible, had joined the Young Men's Mission Association, and taught a class. He confided to his diary:

> *Oh how often since his death, have I wished that he had lived to see me what I now hope I am—a Christian.*

When Principal Weld offered Edward a part-time teaching job in the American School with the privilege of attending Trinity College, his brother's Alma Mater, he accepted with alacrity. His home background had naturally prepared him for the teaching. He was especially pleased to be on the staff the day he stood bareheaded with the faculty and watched the unveiling of a monument on the school's campus in memory of its first principal. The concluding lines of an original poem recited by Mary Peet, daughter of the principal of the New York Institute for the Deaf, expressed his own reaction:

> *His spirit lingering near,*
> *May be reflected here,*
> *In silent hearts, inspiring works of love.*

Edward marched in the Presentation Day procession of Trinity College. His brother Thomas had come from New York to attend the graduation. The brothers recalled that other Presentation Day, fourteen years before, but their positions were now reversed. Eddie was now the black-robed figure, Thomas the one standing on the curb. Yet, in a way they were marching hand in hand, as their father had foreseen. Edward had accepted a full-time teaching position in the American School; now both were working for the deaf.

Edward had at last become his father's son. His father's goal of higher education for the deaf had become his goal. But how to bring it about?

And then the opening came. It was so small an opening that it required a telescope of years to see the end result, a college for the deaf. But Edward had the proper lens. He was asked by Amos Kendall, a great humanitarian, to be superintendent of a new elementary school for the deaf and blind in the nation's capital, an ideal place, he thought, for the special college. He accepted the position on condition that the usual section in the school's by-laws, limiting pupil attendance to a certain number of years, be omitted.

If he couldn't bring about higher education from the top, he would creep up on it from the bottom. With the attendance hazard removed, he could lead his pupils not only through the elementary grades, but on through high school. Then, and his pulse quickened with the strategy, he would present the need of his pupils for college education.

The omission was granted, and Edward became superintendent of the Columbia Institution for the Deaf and Dumb. "I feel I have at last come into my inheritance," he wrote in his diary.

Sophia accepted the position of matron in the new school. Her queenly, yet gentle dignity and experience helped to offset her son's youth and inexperience. Edward was twenty years old.

Viewing his surroundings from a second-story veranda, Edward tried to picture the future. The present landscape revealed a domeless capitol building, a little more than a mile away, where President Buchanan had presided over the nation a little more than four months. The homes of the sixty thousand inhabitants of the city of Washington bordered for the most part on ungraded streets that would be muddy quagmires when it rained. But the rains, inconsiderate of streets, kept the commons between the school and the government buildings green for the grazing cows, goats, and geese.

He watched his nine deaf pupils as they played in the schoolyard. Were these nine the nucleus of his college? Would these grounds and two poorly built frame houses grow into a beautifully landscaped campus with brick buildings of modern architecture? If so, how long would it take?

And then it was 1864, seven years since the opening of Columbia Institution. Many changes had taken place. The school boasted a two and a half story brick building. A new president, Abraham Lincoln, presided in the still domeless capitol building over a nation engaged in civil war.

The school's campus had become a military camp. Three thousand soldiers drank from its wells. A wing of the school was used for a part-time hospital. Sophia and the students scraped lint and made bandages. Flags waved, and fifes shrilled "The Girl I Left Behind Me," as soldiers marched in the dusty streets.

In spite of the confusion, seven deaf boys had completed their preparatory work for college. Edward reasoned that the scholastic as well as the military front should advance. He introduced a bill before Congress asking that Columbia Institution be given the authority to confer college degrees. The bill passed, and on April 8, 1864, was signed by gaunt, weary President Lincoln, a president who took time to consider the future of youth handicapped by deafness, even during the emergencies of war.

College education was now available to the deaf! Edward had made his father's dream, and his own, come true. If it hadn't been for the seriousness of the times he would have declared a jubilee celebration, but people accepted even joyful occasions in silence these days. The new college was named National Deaf-Mute College, and the date set for its inaugural service, June 22, 1864.

On the morning of the inauguration, Edward ushered his mother to a vantage seat. Everyone was quite aware that Sophia's attractive personality and example of accomplishment had been an "immense influence (many Congressmen had met her personally) in persuading Congress to establish National Deaf-Mute College." Her children sat beside her, also Laurent Clerc, who seemed a part of the family. They had come to see the fulfillment of a project that had been discussed in the Gallaudet home for years, and to see the youngest member of the home take his oath of office as president of the project.

In his inaugural address Edward paid tribute to both his father and mother. He reviewed his father's years of work, and then smiling turned towards Sophia.

Dr. Gallaudet gave to the world the most convincing proof of his belief that the deaf and dumb could through education be made the social and

159

*intellectual equals of those possessed of all their
faculties, by taking one of his own pupils as his
wife ... She, my mother, whose ears have ever
been closed to the sound of her children's voices ...
now sits before me an intelligent and joyous partic-
ipant in the exercises of the day ..."*

The war ended in 1865. Edward asked his board for
a leave of absence for a trip to Europe. There was a
decision he felt he must make—a decision his father had
been forced to leave unsolved because of the monopoly
schools in England. The decision dealt with the relative
place of oral and manual instruction in schools for the
deaf.

Edward steamed (no slow sailing *Mexico* now) out
of Boston harbor on an April day, fifty-two years after
his father had crossed the Atlantic on a similar mission.
The first school he visited was the English school where
Thomas had met disappointment. No restrictions now!
He was invited to copy the full course of oral instruction, and observe its methods in operation.

From England he went his inquiring way, visiting the
schools for the deaf in Belgium, Switzerland, Italy,
France ... As he entered the doors of the Royal School
for the Deaf and Dumb in Paris, he felt as if he were
on hallowed ground. He wrote in his journal:

. . . in imagination I went back to the days when my father, at just my present age, tarried here and secured for the thousands of mutes in America then unborn, the priceless boon of education. A new sense of the grandeur of his work came over me, a new enthusiasm was enkindled within me.

Edward came home fully convinced, as his father before him, that the "Combined System" was the ideal method of instructing the deaf. "That no student should be compelled to study under any one method but should develop in that which suited his needs." He recommended that more importance be given to oral instruction: "that instruction in artificial speech and lip reading be entered upon at as early an age as possible; that all pupils in our primary department be afforded [this training] until it plainly appears that success is unlikely . . ."

But plans, instruction methods, systems—all were forgotten in the overwhelming developments that had taken place in his absence. An opposition had arisen in Congress with the avowed purpose of crushing the whole collegiate undertaking. Again the age-old arguments that Thomas had met, were brought out of their graves: "supporting a college for the deaf out of taxpayers' money is unwarranted and extravagant; let the

163

money be spent on the education of those who have all their faculties; if God ordained . . ."

Edward pitched into the fight. The Huguenot and Puritan blood in his veins ran hot against such ignorant injustice. A fierce loyalty to his students and his father drove him on. Sleep was not in his program.

In the final outcome, the fate of the college hung on the vote of one man in the House to swing a majority decision, the vote of Judge Marshall of Illinois. Edward sat in the House gallery (he had done all he could) and desperately prayed, "Lord give us Judge Marshall. Give us Judge Marshall." The judge, after a thoughtful pause while the opposition tried to dissuade him, picked up the pen and signed his name to the bill. National Deaf-Mute College was saved!

Twenty years, lacking one day, had passed since Edward became superintendent and Sophia matron of the Columbia Institution with its nine deaf and five blind pupils. Sophia spent nine years at the school, and then "boarded around" as she termed her stay with sons and daughters who vied for her presence. Always she had the sunniest room, the most comfortable chair. She was nearing eighty and had spent the winter with Edward's family (he now had six children) and would soon be going north for the summer. "Like the birds," she laughingly spelled.

That afternoon Edward had taken her to the city to have new glasses fitted. They would be ready on the morrow. In the evening the family recounted the day's happenings, Sophia taking an active part. At eight o'clock the children signed "good night" to grandma. Edward and his wife went to call on the school physician, and Sophia retired to her room. She donned her long sleeved beruffled nightgown, read a passage of Scripture, and kneeled to pray beside the bed, as was her custom since Thomas had taught her to pray when she came to the American School at nineteen.

When Edward and his wife came home much later, they found her kneeling there. She would not need the new glasses on the morrow nor on any other morrow. She had suffered a stroke.

After funeral services in National Deaf-Mute College, Edward took his mother to Hartford for burial. Sons, daughters, grandchildren, relatives, and friends boarded the train along the way. Services were again held in old Center Church. Children from the American School filed by the casket, each placing a flower upon it. Once more a funeral procession wound its way to the Gallaudet plot in Cedar Hill Cemetery, and Sophia was buried beside Thomas who had preceded her by twenty-six years.

It was while daughters Catherine and Alice were caring for their mother's personal things that they found in her desk the packet of letters written by their father before his and Sophia's marriage. The pink ribbon with which the letters were tied "forever and always" had disintegrated during the treasured keeping. The girls carefully placed the packet in a keepsake box along with Thomas's diaries and the book of debates written at Yale College.

The Centennial year marking Thomas' birth, December 10, 1887, had arrived. To commemorate it Edward Miner published a biography of his father, *The Life of Thomas Hopkins Gallaudet LL.D.* He and Peter Wallace installed a memorial window in Center Church honoring their father's work as chaplain of the Retreat. The window was unveiled at a Gallaudet family reunion.

The National Association of the Deaf held a "Gallaudet Centennial Jubilee" in Faneuil Hall, Boston, the week end of December tenth. Among the events were a grand promenade, tableaux, banquet, masquerade march, singing in signs by deaf children, oral singing by hearing children of deaf-mute parents, orations ... Edward could almost hear his father's questioning comment, could he have been present, "All this fanfare

FRIEND
TEACHER
BENEFACTOR

over a man doing his simple duty, and making a lot of mistakes while doing it?"

The most significant event of the centennial was the voting of a bronze statue of Thomas Hopkins Gallaudet to be placed on the campus of National Deaf-Mute College. Already more than half the necessary funds had been raised. The work was commissioned to Daniel Chester French, sculptor of the Minute Man, at Concord Bridge.

The statue was eventually unveiled on June 26, 1889 before a convention of three hundred alumni. It shows Thomas seated in an old-fashioned three-cornered chair, nine-year-old Alice Cogswell standing by his side. With his right hand he shows her how to form the letter A of the manual alphabet, and looks down at her with sympathy and encouragement. Her wistful face is turned toward his with wonder and the dawn of understanding. On the base of the monument are the words:

FRIEND
TEACHER
BENEFACTOR

Edward was satisfied that full honors had been paid his father, but the college alumni had still another suggestion. A petition was submitted by them to the Board of Directors, asking that the name National Deaf-Mute College, a constant reminder of the students' handicap, be changed to Gallaudet College, "in grateful recognition of the man who founded deaf-mute instruction in America."

It was hinted that the name "Gallaudet College" would include Edward Miner Gallaudet as well, but he would have none of it. His answer was that of the essayist Emmerson: "An Institution is the lengthened shadow of one man." That "shadow" was his father.

Memorials of silver, stone, glass, and bronze; tributes in books, orations, and poems have been dedicated to Thomas Hopkins Gallaudet. But the greatest monuments, and the most lasting memorials, are the generations of deaf youth who, because of available education, have achieved their rightful places in society and the professions.

And it all began with a Yankee boy of Connecticut who, in spite of small stature, frail health, and weak eyes, dared to dream dreams.

BIBLIOGRAPHY

Bibliography

SPECIAL SOURCES:

Department of Manuscripts, Library of Congress
  Diaries, Debates, Letters, Accounts, and Will of
  Thomas Hopkins Gallaudet
  Occasionals and Memoirs of Edward Miner Gallaudet
Rare Book Collection, Library of Congress
  Sophia Gallaudet by Amos G. Draper

BOOKS:

Barnard, Henry—*A Tribute to the Rev. Thomas H.
  Gallaudet LL.D.* (1852)
Bender, Ruth E., Ph.D.—*The Conquest of Deafness*
  (1960)
Boatner, Maxine Tull, Ph.D.—*Voice of the Deaf, A
  Biography of Edward M. Gallaudet* (1959)
Bowditch, Dexter Franklin, Litt.D.—*Yale Biographies
  and Annals* (1805, 1815)

BIBLIOGRAPHY

Cresson, Margaret French—*Journey into Fame*, pp. 148, 149, 156, 157 (1947)

Fay, Edward Allen, Ph.D.—*Histories of American Schools for the Deaf* (1817-1893)

Gallaudet, Edward Miner—*The Life of Thomas Hopkins Gallaudet* (1888)

————, *A History of the Columbia Institution for the Deaf* (1912)

Humphrey, Rev. Heman D.D.—*Life and Labors of the Rev. Thomas Gallaudet* (1857)

Syle, Henry Winter, M.A.—*The First Great Educator of the Deaf in America* (1887)

RELATED BOOKS AND BACKGROUND MATERIAL:

Baird, Charles W.—*History of the Huguenot Emigration to America*, V. I, pp. 251-253, 301

Beals, Carleton—*Our Yankee Heritage* (1955)

Chamberlin, General Joshua L. LL.D.—*Universities and Their Sons* (1898)

Earle, Mrs. Alice—*Dress at the Turn of the Century* (1903)

Federal Writers' Project—*Connecticut*

Fiedler, Miriam Forster—*Deaf Children in a Hearing World* (1952)

Heckman, Helen Elizabeth—*My Life Transformed* (1928)

Jenkins, Stephen—*The Old Boston Post Road* (1913)

Keller, Helen—*The Story of My Life* (1954)

Lee, W. Storrs—*The Yankees of Connecticut* (1957)

BIBLIOGRAPHY

Marlowe, George Francis—*Coaching Roads of Old New England* (1947)

AGAZINES AND PAPERS:

arrett, Mary—"Ten Days with the Deaf and Dumb" *Harper's Magazine* (1873) 47:496

Boatner, Maxine Tull—"Gallaudet the Builder," *Gallaudet College Bulletin* Vol. 3, No. 1

Cortissoz, Royal—"New Figures in Literature and Art," *Atlantic Monthly*, Feb. 1895

Peet, H. P.—"Education of the Deaf and Dumb," *North American Review*, (1858) 87:352-357

Gallaudet Reunion—*Hartford Courant*, July 3, 5, 1887

Wainwright, Rev. J. W.—"Institution at Hartford for Instructing the Deaf and Dumb," *North American Review*, 1818, 7:127

Doctor, Powrie Vaux, Ph.D. "Amos Kendall, Nineteenth Century Humanitarian," *Gallaudet College Bulletin* Vol. 7, No. 1

———, "A Deaf Boy Grows Up in the U.S.A.," *Gallaudet College Bulletin* Vol. 7, No. 2

———, Communication With The Deaf: A Guide for Parents of Deaf Children" (1963)

MERICAN ANNALS OF THE DEAF:

merican School, List of Pupils to 1852, 4: 201-236

———, Visit by President Monroe, 47: 217

———, Use of Manual Alphabet, 39: 63

———, What is the "Combined System"? 40: 31-35

75

BIBLIOGRAPHY

American Schools, Employment of Graduates, 31: 290-292

Brace, Julia, Biographical sketch by James Russell Lowell, 17: 64

———, Notice of her Death, 29: 331

Brown, Thomas, Biographical sketch by Wm. M. Chamberlain, 31: 204-210

Gallaudet, Sophia, Biographical sketch by Amos G. Draper, 22: 170-183

———, Biographical sketch by Edmund Booth, 26: 202

Gallaudet, Thomas Hopkins, Biographical sketch by H. P. Peet, 4: 65-77

———, Biographical sketch by Henry Barnard, 4: 81-136

———, Contract with Clerc, 24: 115-117

———, Married Life, 22: 173-179

———, Unveiling of Painting, 26: 195

———, Gallaudet Reunion (Memorial Window) 32: 240-242

———, Centennial Celebration (1887), 32: 207

———, Centennial Oration by Isaac Lewis Peet, 33: 43-54

———, Statue at Washington—Edmund Booth, 27: 180, 181

———, Statue at Washington—Edmund Booth, 32: 201, 202

———, Statue at Washington—Edmund Booth, 34: 230, 299, 300

————, Statue at Washington—Edmund Booth, 35: 82

————, Statue at Washington—Edmund Booth, 40: 167

Loring, George, Biographical sketch by Royal Cortissoz, 5: 40-45

Spafford, Fisher Ames, Biographical sketch by Robert Patterson, 22: 215-219

BOOKS FOR CHILDREN AND YOUTH BY THOMAS HOPKINS GALLAUDET

Adam to Jacob (1838)

Child's Book of Bible Stories (1834)

Child's Book on Repentance (1834)

Child's Book on the Soul (1830, 1836, 1852)

Child's Picture Defining and Reading Book (1835)

David to Rehoboam (1834)

History of Jonah (1833)

History of Joseph (1833)

History of Moses (1850)

Life of Josiah (1837)

Scripture Biography, 11 v. (1856)

Youth's Book of Natural Theology (1834)

BOOKS BY THOMAS HOPKINS GALLAUDET AND REV. HORACE HOOKER

Family and School Dictionary

Practical Spelling Book